AM I A GOOD GIRL YET?

Carolyn Bramhall

MONARCH
BOOKS

Oxford, UK, and Grand Rapids, Michigan, USA

First published in 2005 by Monarch Books
(a publishing imprint of Lion Hudson plc),
Mayfield House, 256 Banbury Road, Oxford OX2 7DH.
Tel: +44 (0) 1865 302750   Fax: +44 (0) 1865 302757
Email: monarch@lionhudson.com
www.lionhudson.com

Distributed by:
UK: Marston Book Services Ltd, PO Box 269,
Abingdon, Oxon OX14 4YN;
USA: Kregel Publications, PO Box 2607,
Grand Rapids, Michigan 49501.

ISBN-13: 978-1-85424-724-7 (UK)
ISBN-10: 1-85424-724-7 (UK)
ISBN-13: 978-0-8254-6100-2 (USA)
ISBN-10: 0-8254-6100-6 (USA)

British Library Cataloguing Data
A catalogue record for this book is available
from the British Library.

Printed in Great Britain.

This book is dedicated to John, my husband and best friend, and to my two amazing children, Amy and Luke. I am so proud of you, the three most precious people in my life.

As you live this new life, we pray that you will be strengthened from God's boundless resources, so that you will find yourselves able to pass through any experience and endure it with joy. You will even be able to thank God in the midst of pain and distress because you are privileged to share the lot of those who are living in the light. For we must never forget that he rescued us from the power of darkness, and re-established us in the kingdom of his beloved Son. For it is by his Son alone that we have been redeemed and have had our sins forgiven.

Colossians 1:11–14 (Phillips Translation)

Acknowledgments

It has been a great privilege to have been loved and supported by many remarkably faithful and loving individuals who demonstrate that the church of Jesus Christ is alive and working out the kingdom of God. My heartfelt thanks go to so many wonderful people that I am not going to attempt to mention individuals here. Many names are in the book, others are not. They know, I know and God knows who they are. My prayer is that our God of freedom and good surprises may abundantly bless them.

Some names and places have been changed to protect identities, but everything written here is as true as I am able to recollect or piece together. In order to record my story as accurately as possible I have delved into reams of therapy notes, journals, photographs, alters' artwork, interviews with friends and the numerous letters that crossed the Atlantic while we were apart as a family. Much of the material about the therapy sessions comes from the video and audio records we kept about that time, so the conversations recounted here are largely direct transcripts.

I am particularly grateful to the Lord for the Freedom in Christ material and the team who have, and continue to, faithfully teach those vital truths. God's word is releasing, His grace unchanging and His love healing. Ultimately all the glory must go to Him.

Contents

Part 3

Foreword

I have had the great privilege of helping people all over the world resolve their personal and spiritual conflicts and find their freedom in Christ. I have seen God set captives free and bind up the broken hearts of those who have been abused. I have never been more convinced in my life that Jesus is the answer, and the truth of God's word will set us free to be all that God called us to be.

I have seen God's children overcome depression, anxiety disorders, sexual and chemical addiction, and abuse of all kinds, but the most difficult cases have been those who have been subjected to satanic ritual abuse.

Many of those who have been subjected to such atrocities have to resort to dividing up their mind and compartmentalizing their pain in order to live with the painful truth of their abuse. That ability is called "Dissociation"; it is a God-given ability and is a severe defence mechanism. In the presence of abuse, the person dissociates, which allows them to develop somewhat normally with no memory of the incident. However, another portion of themselves was present and has memories of the atrocities.

If you have never seen a person switch from one personality to another, it is hard to believe that such a phenomenon could even happen. Some personalities can be quite similar and often go undetected when an alternate personality comes out, but others are radically different. Multiple Personality Disorder was the common designation, but presently and professionally the condition is known as Dissociative Identity Disorder (DID).

I conducted a conference in Texas and returned to the same area a year later. A professional counsellor was using our discipleship counselling approach for her clients, but had come across one who seemed to resist her efforts. She asked if I would meet together with her and her client, which I did. Five minutes into our session, the client arose angrily from her chair and said, "I am sick and tired of you trying to get rid of me." The counsellor said, "See, there it is," believing it was a demon. I said, "That is not a demon, that is another personality."

The common error of the church is to try getting rid of personalities thinking they are demons, and many professional counsellors who lack theological training try to integrate demons into the personality of their clients, thinking they are alternate personalities. To complicate matters, the victims often don't know one from the other, since both sound like "voices" in their head. Such clients pose a real challenge, since resolution requires spiritual discernment, a working knowledge of Scripture and an understanding of dissociation.

The "religious" nature of the problem leaves secular psychologists stumped. They sometimes express that the church should probably be involved, but they don't believe in the church, and know nothing of the healing power we have in Christ. Consequently, they seldom if ever see the total integration that comes when God is the Wonderful Counsellor. Here we have the story of someone who has come to know complete wholeness because people were both open to the truth of the word of God and listened to and believed Carolyn's story. Therefore she was led into an understanding of who she was as a divided personality, and who she now is in Christ. That latter truth brought her complete freedom.

At first I thought DID was extremely rare, but as I started travelling the country in the early eighties I was encountering many pastors and counsellors who were struggling to help these dear people. Those who make it have learned who they are in Christ, and have assumed their own responsibility for wholeness. Through genuine repentance and faith in God they learn to stand complete in Christ, and clearly recognize that Jesus has set them free and bound up their broken heart.

This story illustrates the fact that when the truth is allowed to penetrate every part of a personality in spite of extreme inner pain and fragmentation, and God is allowed to work his work of grace, healing and wholeness will result. Carolyn is now a powerful instrument in the hands of God to help others walk through the journey of recovery in Christ, because she knows first hand that the truth really does set people free from the bondage of sin's ravages. This account will bring hope both to those who are attempting to understand a client or church member, and to those who are themselves tormented by voices and inner anguish.

All this, because he who is in us is greater than he who is in the world. Praise God from whom all blessings flow.

Dr Neil T. Anderson
Founder of Freedom In Christ Ministries,
President of Discipleship Counseling Ministries
(www.discipleshipcounselingministries.org)

Exposure

Dare I ?
Dare I take the risk?
Dare I expose my living-weary heart for you to scrutinize?
If you touch me I hurt.
My hurt is sacred.
Only the few are permitted to glimpse –
Will dare to glimpse
At the vulnerable mix of pain and joy called "me".
But supposing, just supposing
I let you feel the pain –
That wrenching of sinews, heart-tearing agony,
Called fear, self-doubt.
Supposing I let you peep at shattered dreams;
Hope snuffed out – but shining yet.
Maybe you have a caress, balm-breath, oil of love.
Maybe, just maybe, you can help loose the suffocating,
screaming bondage
And I could breathe again.
Maybe, just maybe, you can lift
The steel-cold weight of self-condemnation,
And allow waves of friendship
Bathe the thirsty shore of my tired self-worth,
Washing it into life.
Thank you.

Thank you for allowing me
To allow myself to hurt,
Crushed, but not destroyed,
To show you who I am.

Introduction

High-pitched screams explode into the air, unrelenting, shot through with blind terror. A wounded animal? A torture chamber?

A calm voice interrupts the heart-chilling cries, reassuring my reluctant, listening ears that the victim is in a safe place. But her fearful trauma haunts me, echoing in every straining sinew of my mind.

I switch the tape off and lean back on the cushions of the over-stuffed armchair to better ponder what I have just heard. Those screams belonged to a small child – just a child – mercilessly gripped in the vice of uncontrollable and devastating fear. What atrocity would have caused such a violent outburst? What unmentionable evil warped her budding innocence? Can I bear to hear more?

Trembling, I stretch over and turn the tape on again, pushing the limits of my endurance to listen to more of this nerve-wringing tirade. I lean forward, muscles tense, temples throbbing, mouth dry. At last the screams fade to a whimper, as a steady male voice soothes the young victim. His words unruffled, constant. Her small, high whine gradually lulls to a moan, pathetic and painful. Weary wails struggle, exhausted, from the tape player on the coffee table in front of me: "No more... no more... no, no more...". Silence.

He continues his balm of words: "You are just remembering, just remembering; I'm here. You are safe now. That was all a long time ago. It's all just a memory. No one is going to hurt you any more. No one. You're safe now."

My unconscious sigh of relief jolts me back to the present and once again I stoop to switch off the tape, my shaking spirit daring my mind to consider the ghastly implications of what I have just heard.

Will that child ever be able to describe what she has seen? Will she ever be allowed to express what was done to her? Will she ever be able to feel joy, freedom?

And who is that child?

I struggle intensely with that last question, horribly aware that I know the answer, though even yet desperately clinging onto the breaking branch of my unbelief. I know her well – oh, how well I know her! I have heard her screams often.

That child is me.

Part 1

Chapter
1

Secrets

I had a secret. Well, don't we all? Skeletons in our cupboards? Only mine was less like a skeleton and more like a full-blooded person, alive and kicking lustily. In fact there were more than one, my cupboard was noisy and bursting at the seams. For years I didn't know the secret myself, I knew there were skeletons, of course. I just didn't know what, or who, they were. Then when I did, I felt embarrassed. And wrong, like you do when you have burst in on somebody dressing and caught them unawares. I caught myself still struggling to get internally dressed; I was not ready to see what I saw. Others got to know, and my seeping, creeping shame turned to horror – until I learnt to recognize love and realized there was no judgment in their eyes. I was not condemned for who I was after all, only seen as different.

What happened was that, for reasons you will later understand, my personality became fragmented into many parts in order to help me cope with living. I lived a number of different lives, all still me. So it required great effort to haul my foot forward and continue. What great things I could have done with my life if I hadn't had these secrets! How powerful I could have been! What amazing heights I could have reached... but no, I had to drag this thing, this thorn in the flesh, this knowledge of the past, round with me until I was too tired to carry on. I was ready to give up, throw in the towel, stamp my foot and refuse to play the game of life any more. Then something happened… other people came on the scene; people who were willing to know and still love me.

You may, of course, decide not to believe all that I tell you. It is rather bizarre, and some of you may rather too easily discount things you cannot explain or identify with. My request is that you at least consider it all carefully. I am not as odd as you may think, and God in his infinite wisdom and tenderness has turned unspeakable evil into a kaleidoscope of hope.

Because my multi-dimensional personality contained colours I didn't much like, life seemed easier when I wasn't aware of it. Until one day somebody else detected it – a flicker of their light caught a fragment of my colour and the secret was out.

I want to tell you my story now because I am no longer afraid, no longer ashamed at my odd mix of colours. They were and are mine. Yours will be different. Maybe just as varied, just as diverse, but different. For years I carried the story of my past round with me like some dreadful, unconfessed sin. Now I don't see it as unwanted baggage, unwillingly heaved around on my aching back. It is part of the wonderful story of my redemption, and in turn part of the unified, magnificent, boundless chronicle of how God has delivered all humankind from our tarnished and sorry past, and joyfully deposited those of us who are willing into a kingdom where light and beauty and the unrestrained fountain of life reign.

Some people have, along the way, discovered my secret of a multiple-me and became frightened. Some have been shocked, others repelled. Many ran towards me to embrace and cover me. I have been pitied, admired, resented, loved, hated, blamed and pampered. Some have disbelieved me, most haven't. I have been manipulated, ill-used and exploited. But mostly enclosed, surrounded, protected and loved. In it all I saw myself as a helpless victim of the whims and fancies of others, one moment held with great care, the next discarded, kicked away like yesterday's newspaper.

The Jesuit priest John Powell once wrote a book with the telling title *Why Am I Afraid To Tell You Who I Am?* It was subtitled "I am afraid to tell you who I am because you may not like who I am and it's all that I have". Today I am telling you who I am. I take a risk – you may not like what you see, what you come to learn about me. But it is a risk I am prepared to take because I believe we have more things in common than we have differences. I believe that we share the same basic fears and longings. That's why Jesus could say he knows "all men" for we – including us ladies – are all so similar. When I read about others I see myself. I write with a certain assumption that you will meet yourself, or if this is too scary at least someone you know, in these pages.

I now choose to allow you to peer into the cupboard and look at my secret skeletons; to screw up your eyes and turn my kaleidoscope and view the multicoloured marvel that God has made called the human mind. For it is he who has amazingly put me together, not by some unexplainable wham! bam! stars-in-your-eyes, trumpet-sounding miracle. But by the persistent and gentle renewing of my mind by the Holy Spirit, as I chose to believe what God has said about me in his word. There was no great moment. The sign and the wonder happened as God's people loved me enough to see me through the slog of choosing the truth, day in and day out, through the good times and the bad, without fanfare. And it is the truth that has set me free. Today I am whole and can, without shame or fear, tell you my story.

* * *

I got born, like you did. All was reasonably well for a short while; doting parents and adoring aunts made all the right noises at this cute bundle of flesh, blood and damp nappy. It is difficult to say when, where or how things started to go pear-shaped, but my life did not turn out as one would have expected. But then, do things ever? The good thing was that God, in his infinite wisdom and awesome power, not to mention his sense of the sublimely ridiculous, knew exactly what was happening and held me firmly in the palm of his hand. That was the beginning of a number of "God things" that kept me alive and kicking even to this very day.

Chapter
2

A Child

Ordinary things can sparkle in even the darkest of minds; the little things that insist on spreading their light, borne of their innate purity. If you looked hard enough in the blackened room that was my childhood there could be seen some glimmers of goodness. No, more than glimmers, vast rays of beauty that, if allowed to spread their bright and shining fingers of hope throughout my young mind, would bathe my days in the splendour of the present; the goodness of the now. God has gifted children with that enviable ability of being able to enjoy the moment as they experience it, that delicious taste of heaven that can outshine and completely engulf the trauma of the past or trepidation for the future. Simple moments. Pure. Like the complete and utter warmth of feeling strong arms wrapped lovingly around that small body that is yours, or the colour of the sky just before bedtime, or the sound of sparrows arguing.

I was a child once...

There was a swing. I remember it, standing among the forlorn and spineless hydrangeas – sometimes blue, sometimes pink, at the bottom of our narrow garden (which was mostly concrete for dad's car). There it hung, between the half-drunk shed and a wall that was whitewashed and nearly reached the sky. But it was still only a wall. The Big White Wall ran the whole length of our house in Chelsea Street and was supposed to separate us from the car factory right next door. But it was useless. It didn't do anything to keep out the noise. Ear-splitting whines and drills. Then more whines and more drills, like a very loud dentist's drill. From dawn to dusk, my mum said. She once taped them on my little tape recorder and took it to the police station. She wrote lots of cross letters. But nothing changed, they still kept making car bodies with noisy drills. I played out the back anyway and pretended the bangs were from a blacksmith hammering shoes for horses in the olden days. I didn't like the noise either, but I didn't cry like my mum. Even in the night cars came and stopped with a horrid screech outside and woke you up sometimes. I wondered why people came to an empty factory all shut up in the spooky darkness; I wondered what they did there.

The swing's smooth wooden seat hung on ropes woven by dad. He was clever like that; he could do things with bits of rope and tie knots to be proud of. That was on account of him being in the Navy in the war. He also learnt how to cook dinner in a storm when the sea was up and down and the air was full of fog. So we had our swing and I put my teddy on it and pushed him high in the sky. I don't remember going on it myself. Don't know why. Just didn't. I'm not very good about strings and ropes.

Our house was a busy sort of house. Granny was in charge, even in charge of mum and dad. And, of course, my sister, Kate. Granny sat like the queen in the front room where she and granddad lived, and every day loads of aunties (she was in charge of them too) came to drink cups of tea with them, and talk about people in the village and the price of rhubarb. I wasn't interested, and would tiptoe past the front room after school before they realized I was back and wanted me to go in and kiss them and drink tea and tell them things. I wasn't interested. I wanted to go up to my bedroom and read, or go and play in the fields we called the "Moor" at the end of the road and be quiet with myself. The aunties didn't understand about being quiet with yourself, or catching minnows in the river or watching the sun go down. They didn't understand about much to do with me, and I didn't want them to. They once took a bit of interest when I planted flowers out the back next to the concrete. That was when dad helped me to dig a pond and we filled it with water and I paid for goldfish out of my pocket money. They said it was very nice, dear. But I wasn't really bothered about what they said anyway. It was a happy thing to do, and I waited for the shoots to peep their heads out of the ground in the spring, and watch the plants grow green and strong. I liked that a lot. It made me feel big on the inside.

We shared a room, Kate and me. We were twins but you would never know it because she was prettier than me and taller and had fair hair. She was different from me, too. She played with different friends and we liked different things. She was kind of normal. I wasn't, 'least I never thought so.

But sharing a room with Kate was OK. Then when we got bigger I had the bottom of the old bunk beds somebody gave us, and would annoy her by pushing her mattress up with my feet and she would bounce up and down when she was trying to go to sleep. Then she would get cross and shout for mum. I wanted to have the top bunk but mum said I kept falling out in the night, so I couldn't. I wasn't very good with nights. I didn't like to go to sleep very much, so had to stay and watch the darkness for a long time. Just in case. Once a big, fat beetle ran across my face and it was thunder and lightning outside and mum said he had just come in to shelter from the rain. But I wish he hadn't wanted to come and walk around on me.

I always wanted to be a teacher when I grew up. Then I

could tell little children things that they would want to learn, and they would all listen to me. Nobody else listened to me. I would be very kind, the kindest teacher ever. When you are a teacher you get to read books and talk to people who are clever, and learn more things from them. I couldn't think of anything better than to be a teacher. Except perhaps a writer. I could be a writer and write stories and use interesting words that tell people what is going on in my head. Then people would read what I had written, and I could write things down to help them understand what is going on in their heads too. Only I could never be a teacher or a writer because I wouldn't ever be clever enough. All the aunties and my mum cleaned other people's houses, so I would probably end up like them. At least, that's what they said. But I really didn't want to be like them. I didn't want to clean fireplaces and wash clothes and put them through the wringer and get wrinkly hands and drink tea and talk about the price of rhubarb. I wanted to learn things and be kind.

School was OK I suppose, except when I felt poorly, which was quite a lot. Then I would cry and cry and couldn't do any-thing else. Mrs Croft from the office would hold my hand and walk me home, and Mum would get me stuff from the doctor, which meant I would soon be better and have to go to school again. When I felt poorly it was all too much. Even school. I would have to talk to the other children, which is all right when you are feeling well, but not when you feel weird and sort of somewhere else and are too tired to talk. I was always too tired. They were all too loud and wanted to know things that I didn't want to tell them. I have to be a good girl, see.

Usually I was a good girl. It doesn't pay to be anything else. It's best if the teachers like you, and think you are a nice person, even if you're not. Then they don't bother you or pick you out in front of everyone else, and make you feel silly and go red and stutter. I tried my very, very hardest to be a good girl, and not be picked out. Once, something went wrong. I don't know what I did, I never did find out, but I had to go upstairs to the head mistress' office. You only have to go up there when you've been really naughty. I sometimes wonder what I did that was naughty. My inside was banging really loudly and I had to knock on the door and wait until she said to come in. It was funny to find her office so clean and tidy, not like the classrooms downstairs. It smelt clean and wooden, like just-sharpened pencils, and the books on the shelves were all standing upright and nice and straight, and her desk had a clear space in front of where she sat, with a white pad so that she could write things down. Her green skirt had straight pleats in it, just like they are in the shop, and her blouse had a big bow just under her chin, and no wrinkles. Not like my white school blouse with the curled up collar and fuzzy cuffs. She seemed much smaller in her office than when she was standing in assembly in front of everyone. Kind of warmer. I wanted to stay there with her, especially when I realized she wasn't going to shout at me. She just said not to be naughty again. I wished the headmistress could be my mum. She would talk to me and know things, and be strong and would never cry and I could copy what she did and be clever.

Then I came down the stairs. Luckily no one was in the big hall so no one saw me walk down. It was really funny creeping into the classroom when everyone else was already there and doing things.

Everything in school smells of wax crayons and chalk and wooden puzzles and the front desks are covered in white dust. When it rains the classroom smells of damp wool and there is wetness in the air that swirls round every time the door opens and the geraniums on the window-sills smell louder than they usually do. At wet play there are comics to read. We are supposed to sit in our usual seats and read quietly but lots of children walk around and talk and shout. Especially the boys. I don't. I always do as I am told even if nobody else does. Because it doesn't pay to be naughty. I have to be good. It's better if you are a good girl. We don't have comics at home because they cost too much, but I can read them at wet play-times. If you look hard through the pile on Miss's desk, and if you're quick and lucky, you can find one that is all about facts and learning, and has about animals and history and things. They're the best ones. But I always feel a bit bad about taking these back to my seat, because these are what rich children have, and children who are clever. They have more pages and have lots of different colours and are not meant for children like me, so I only look at a couple of things in them, ever so quickly, and take care not to wrinkle the pages, then put them back. Tidy, like Miss said. Then I have to make do with silly stories in tatty comics, about girls in short white socks, who play with dogs that wear bows around their necks, and have adventures.

I hate Wednesday afternoons because we have sewing in the big hall. I wish every minute away. The minutes are very long. It's a waste of time – sewing samplers and making draw-string bags that nothing will fit in. I want to be somewhere else. On my own. Instead, I watch the others do it right while I spend ages undoing my stitches. I dread Miss coming to see what I have done because it is always wrong. Supposing she was to ask me why I am doing it wrong. I am so tired that I can hardly see in front of me, so how can I be expected to make fiddly little stitches? But I have to be good and happy and pretend that I can do it. I really want to cry because she might tell me off, and then it would mean I am a naughty girl. But I mustn't. So I will be strong and a good girl and not cry and be a baby.

There are spiders in the girls' toilets. Big fat ones and you have to keep your eyes on them when you are sitting down in case they crawl onto you. I don't like the girls' toilets, so it's best to hang on till home-time. The toilets are outside in the playground. They are cold and smelly and the walls drip with damp even in the summer. When it's raining and the teacher lets you go during lessons because you are desperate you have to run quickly or you get soaked from the rain. It's best not to tell Miss you have wet clothes. It's best not to make a fuss and be picked out or you may not be able to answer her questions and then you go red and it's awful. I'm not very good at answering questions. I forget things.

I was eleven when I started the Guides and was allowed to go to camp even though I wasn't truly a Guide and didn't have a uniform or anything. My sister didn't come, just me. We went to Bracklesham Bay, which was by the seaside. It was cold and windy and the food had bits of grass in it, and our clothes got all wrinkled and smelt like a river. But we sang songs around a campfire at night-time and played rounders in the tufty field. I was really good at getting rounders on account of the grown-ups saying my legs were sturdy. When you have sturdy legs you can run fast. I'm not really very big, see. I could make people laugh because I was ever so much smaller than everyone else and could dodge around the big girls' legs and they liked me and let me sit on their shoulders when we walked to the beach. They made up a song about me, which they sang:

> Red, white and blue, little tiny Carrie
> We all love her too, little tiny Carrie
> She's strong as a pussycat,
> And never will give up,
> That's why Carrie is favourite in the camp.

It was to the tune of "World Cup Willy". I didn't know who World Cup Willy was, but I am still glad they made up that song, because it made me feel good. Well, for a little while anyway. But people are different in Guide camp from what they are in real life, and it wasn't the same when we came back. I would pretend that I didn't mind if they didn't like me any more. I would stand next to other girls when I saw people coming so they would think I was a good girl and had lots of friends.

But in time I did get to be Patrol Leader for the Robins. I was strict. I had to be strict or else no one would take any notice of me on account of my being so small (I was very, very little indeed), and I had to pretend to be important. People like you when you are important. They have to, that's the way it works. When I was twelve the PE teacher measured me because I was smaller than the high jump in PE. I was four foot three inches and my friend Samantha could jump over me. People were always calling me names like "Squirt" and "Midget" and "Baby". I didn't like it but didn't ever let on. They never made me cry because I had to be good. Somebody might see me crying and call me even more names, or they may tell a teacher and then they would ask me questions. It's better to be good.

Sometimes in the summer Dad would go for walks at night with me. We went over the moor and through the buttercup field and past the weir. There was only us. We sometimes heard foxes crying and owls calling with their bubbly hoot. Sometimes Dad wanted to hold my hand even though I was a teenager and teenagers don't usually do that sort of thing with dads. When we came back it was the black of night and I went to bed. I don't know why my dad wanted to take me for walks in the fields at night, but he did.

There are loads of aunties. Every day they come and drink

tea in granny's room, and talk all the time. I'm glad I'm not an aunty, it must be very boring. You have to sit in that hot little room with the fire blazing even when it's warm out, and drink out of cups with saucers that don't match, and eat stale teatime biscuits out of the musty old biscuit barrel. The biscuits were always soft and tasted like crumbly chalk. The coal fire was sort of dusty, and the wind blew the smoke back down the chimney. But nobody batted an eyelid, they didn't even notice the soot on their biscuits. All the aunties are fat and short. Perraps it's cos they ate too many stale biscuits. Mum had six sisters, and I think they are just like the seven dwarfs.

Aunty Cath had a twitch on her shoulder and just when you were not expecting it she would jerk suddenly and her head and shoulder would meet each other. Mum said it was because she had TB in the war and had to stay in something called a sanatorium. They put her bed outside in the fresh air 'cos it was supposed to make her better. I went to the seaside once and saw where the place was, except that it was a broken-down ruin of red bricks with big holes in the roof. The wind was so strong it blew the rain sideways. If Aunty Cath had to lie in bed in that weather it was no wonder she had a twitch.

Aunty Milly was the best aunty. She talked about sensible things because she was a Guider and had to think about tents and badges, which is better for your mind than the price of rhubarb. She didn't go to granny's room every day and when she did she didn't stay long because she had a sensible mind. Aunty Milly had a stutter and took ages to say the first word of the sentence properly. So you had time to guess what the rest of the sentence might be while she battled with the first word. Nobody minded though, because she was important and a Leiutenant. She knew how to make things out of twigs, like gadgets that keep kit bags off the ground and things that keep plastic bowls and stuff tidy. Aunty Milly was so important that she got to stand with the very best leaders at the area Guide events, and wear a special uniform. I got proud because she was my aunty and even when she was with important people she would come and talk to me to let everyone know that I was her niece.

Aunty Bet had no teeth to speak of, unless you count the two yellow pegs on one side of her mouth. Mum said she had never been to a dentist, and I believe her. Her breath smelt like our house did after Mum has cooked cauliflower for dinner. She was deaf like Granny and we had to shout at her because she had never been to a doctor either, and won't go and get a hearing aid. Granny had one that whistled all the time. Sometimes it wasn't switched on properly then one of the aunties would fiddle with it and the squeal was deafening. Add that to all the loud talking and the stirring of tea and the heavy front door opening and closing and the drills going hammer and tongs next door and you understand why I had to go to the moor to be quiet with myself.

The moor was the very best place in all the world. I liked it when I was with my friend Susan, or my cousins, but I liked it better when I was on my own. I once told a cow all about everything and she talked back to me with her big brown eyes, and didn't go away. We found a robin's nest once on the old tree trunk that had fallen across the stream. You could paddle in it, the stream, until it flowed into the big river. I wished we had a different river, because ours had a funny name I kept forgetting and I wanted it to be called Thames or Avon or something famous, but it wasn't, and I had to like it or lump it. If you looked hard at the sky you could pretend you were in Switzerland like Heidi, and one time I looked for so long at the clouds I cried. I wanted to be far away in Switzerland, where there are no factories and no aunties and no concrete instead of a garden, and you can hear the bells on the goats, and eat cheese and see mountains covered in pine trees. One day, when I grow up, I will live in a place like Switzerland with pine trees and mountains and be a million miles away from factories with drills that bore holes in your head. And I will sleep every night in peace and quiet and not be interrupted by someone wanting me to empty Granny's commode.

But anyway, I had the moor, and if you walked into the next field, the one with the old rusty roller in it, you could pretend that you were miles away from home. You could pretend you were on holiday, or in the real countryside, and live in a farmhouse with chickens and ducks outside the door, and a cat on the hearth, and a dog in a kennel in the yard who rounds up the sheep. I dreamt that one day I would marry a farmer and when I came home from being a teacher or a writer all day I would eat the sugary apple pie the cook has made out of apples from our orchard and walk in the fields and feed the animals. It will be bright and sunny, with birds and animals all around me, and grass and trees, and lots of quiet and nobody who interferes or asks questions I don't want to answer. The nights would be really short and full of happy thoughts, and I wouldn't have to wait until the telly was switched off before I read the *Famous Five*.

Chapter
3

A Change

Of course, I was not aware that my mind was splintered, any more than a baby born blind knows that she has been denied a most precious gift that the rest of us have. Only when she becomes aware that others speak of colour and shape, light and dark, depth and form, can she begin to comprehend the difference.

I simply assumed that everyone dealt with life the way I did. At the back of my mind was always a sneaking suspicion that I was different – but that was a feeling I clung to as an asset, it helped my faltering sense of identity, my struggle to figure out who I was and where I was going. I already knew I was different from my sister but couldn't really figure out why. She was she and I was me, and that was that.

Throughout my growing-up years I continued to function with a corporate mind, successfully filtering out all that was unpleasant, fearful, terrible, and ciphering those experiences into separate parts, sending each type of memory, feeling or emotion to the part of me created to hold it. That enabled me to lead a comparatively tranquil internal existence. I did not understand fear, much less terror; I had no concept of anger, never mind rage; and my grasp of anything remotely sexual was virtually nil. All information that smacked of the physically intimate was immediately filed away to the sections whose job it was to manage that kind of thing.

* * *

The alley is dark and I don't want to go down there but I have no choice. Somehow I have to. I have to keep on running. The stitch in my side is stabbing like knives but I mustn't stop. Have to run. Along empty streets, down narrow alleys, past whispering, silhouetted trees flanking wide council-estate streets, the moon playing tag with the racing night-time clouds. Breathlessly I run frantically on, a solitary fugitive, a parody of what my life was to feel like in the long and lonely years ahead.

This didn't happen every night, but sometimes there was an overwhelming compulsion to make an excuse at home and run out into the darkness. I must get away from it, and yet I run towards it. The darkness pursues me, yet I am looking for it.

These confusions all started in earnest when I said that special prayer – when I took the plunge and opened up my whole heart, my whole life to God, the God I knew about but hadn't really met until that day.

At fourteen years old, having shouldered and identified the distant awareness that I was not like other people, I began to look at the inner isolation in which I lived. Fourteen can be a broody age at the best of times. It often tends to be the lot of fourteen-year-olds to become self-contemplative and to prefer to stay behind closed doors for long periods.

My closed doors tended to be rather open ones – the wind and the sky. I could breathe freely in the nearby fields where only the equally broody cows could look on and witness my sullenness and I felt they understood. Only there could I feel private, safe.

It was Valentine's Day. I remember so well the honest blue sky, deep and tranquil, the air cold and clean. I was a figure with a mission, striding down the empty street towards the moor early that February morning. The weak sun hadn't yet melted the frost and the sparkling grass crackled underfoot. I reached the middle of the large meadow, surrounded on three sides by a stream and brown spiky hedgerow, and on the fourth by the distant road. This was a safe place, my place. No one would overhear me here. I peered into the bright blue above me and spoke aloud with all the courage I could muster. "Dear God. I know about you…" I paused and waited, gathering my thoughts. The air was quiet, expectant. So far, so good. Then I took a deep breath, "But God – do you know about me…"

There was no heavenly anthem, no voice. The high and wispy clouds made no comment. But the world stopped. No. It began! The sun was brilliant, warm, real. The grass beneath me was oh! so green, so beautiful. The muddy track with its rills and grooves fascinating, wonderful. The air sang. The trees sang. Everything sang. And I – all within me, every fibre, every muscle, every nerve – sang too. Nothing was changed and yet everything was changed. I had just woken from a deep sleep. I had opened my eyes and found it was morning. I had risen from the dead! I was alive! He knows! God knows!

Suddenly I needed to get home; I had to pray properly, on my knees. I turned and ran – across the field, along the track, over the bridge, across the road, down our little street, through the front door, up the stairs and, with the bedroom door firmly shut, I dropped to my knees. I had to do this in the right way, just to make sure God knew that I was serious about this, more serious than I had ever been about anything in all my life. There on the floor in great earnestness I prayed: "Dear God. Thank you for sending Jesus to die for me. Thank you for forgiving my sins. Please come into my life. Please. Oh! Please. Please. Thank you, oh, thank you, oh, thank you. Thank you. Thank you…"

I now knew that God was real. I didn't just hope it or believe it. I knew it. A kind of bone knowledge. Something deep within me had sprung open, and light had entered. Some recognition, some amazing, unexplainable miracle had occurred and I felt in tune with God. The "Our-Father" God. The heaven-and-earth God. He understands. How wonderful, how glorious, how delicious! How utterly, amazingly, fantastically wow! What a great relief; I am known. The things that nobody else knows, he knows! He knows! He *knows!*

It would be another twenty years before I understood fully why it was so important to me that God knew what others did not. I had no conscious awareness that anything had been amiss in my life. The Lord knew I needed to know, and in his wisdom and kindness he told me.

The following Sunday I decided to go along to church to see what proper Christians were like. People looked posh and hushed. They smiled a lot and were kind and polite. We sang hymns out of old books. But then came the message. That was the best bit. The dishy young pastor knew what he was talking about – he became animated as he spoke about the truth in God's word. He told a story about a man who sold everything he had in order to buy a field that had treasure buried in it. Sensible chap, he knew what he wanted and gave his all in order to get it. I want to be like that.

Living was different after that; I was different; the world was different. I lived in a realm above where I had been before. There was meaning to life, and I was not alone. I was followed and led. I was accompanied and surrounded. I was on a mission – to find more of this God, to understand more; to meet him again and again and again.

I found the courage to think about the future. I was grounded in a world that touched reality; I didn't have to resort to fantasy to colour it with beauty, it had been there all along. I had a present, a now, that was bearable – even good. It just had to come out somehow – the amazing fact that I was

alive in a beautiful world. I wrote poems and songs and prose
– it all tumbled out for weeks, no months. Everybody ought to
know about this. Why is it such a secret, that Jesus, the Son of
the living God, is alive and meets with ordinary people? How
come churchy people aren't telling everyone they meet? They
must be crazy not to be going crazy about this. I did! Of
course I did – God knows it all, so we don't have to worry. He
knows about us, and loves us anyway. That has to be the
biggest, best news the world has ever known. How come
everyone isn't buzzing with it? I don't understand.

My personal mission to make sure all within my acquain-
tance knew about Jesus, lasted several years. The first point of
impact was at home. Mum rang the pastor of the little Baptist
church we went to (my sister and I were sent to Sunday school
every week from four-years-old). She asked him crossly, "For
goodness sake tell us what on earth has got into Carrie? She
insists on doing the washing-up and driving us round the
bend with her singing and bouncing about the house. Is this
some obsession, or just a teenage phase that will pass?"
Within a few weeks of my "conversion", for that is what it
technically was, though I didn't know the jargon, I had helped
all five of my Sunday school class to pray that prayer and
know the real God. We used to hold hands and skip around
the church hall after the service, singing the new choruses we
were learning from *Youth Praise*, and being a general nuisance.
I still could not understand why my joy was not shared. "I am
gobsmacked with God – 'Godsmacked!' Why aren't you?"

The excitement, the freshness of experiencing something
so outside of myself, was wonderfully good. The conviction
that I had been touched by the divine, like stumbling on treasure hidden in a field, completely changed the way I looked
at myself and the world. This new awareness of God rapidly
opened like a daisy in the sunshine, and I felt my new per-

sonhood blossoming under the protective leaves of Philip Greenslade, my prayerful pastor and his gentle wife. His fine teaching and deep love for the Scriptures gave me a lasting legacy no amount of money could buy. I owe much of my own delight in God's word to his example.

Of course, there was now no question about what I would do when I left school. I had, before that Valentine's Day "explosion", seriously considered giving up ideas of being a writer or teacher, and going into horticulture. My world was full of nature – my little patch in the back garden had now extended to a portion of an allotment too. I revelled in digging my fingers into the rich brown earth, and feeling sure that life would come from it again. The moor was my playground and my friends were the trees and birds there. I felt safer out there than at home, and I could escape any unpleasant thoughts when I immersed myself in the business of getting my hands dirty and growing things.

But now it had all changed. Gardening could wait. This was far more important – I needed to become a missionary or something. This good news had to be told, I was going to tell it, and that was that. Nothing that anyone could say would dissuade me, at home, at school or anywhere else. My transfer to the Grammar school in order to take "A" Levels only strengthened my conviction, for they welcomed me with open arms as someone mug enough to lead the Junior Christian Union. Here was a group of eleven to thirteen-year-olds from highly professional homes – very different to my own background – who wanted "Sunday school" at school. They got me instead. But I revelled not only in their malleability, but also in my new role of pastoral counsellor, Bible teacher and mother all rolled into one. With my (dreadful) guitar skills and (sketchy) Bible knowledge we muddled through together until I was elevated to the grave and awesome distinction of leader of the Senior Christian Union. Heady stuff.

One day a bouncy, happy chappy called Gerald Coates came and gave a meeting on the playing field. Half the school were there – it wasn't often we saw a male of any sort, let alone one so vibrant and energetic and, well, happy. I stood at the edges, trying to see and hear what was going on, though failing on all counts, not being very blessed in the height department. Apparently loads went forward to become Christians, and also experience something else. Somehow my status as leader of the Junior Christian Union didn't usher me into the hallowed presence of the "in" crowd swarming around this important figure, and consequently I missed all the action. All the girls were buzzing with talk of something called the "baptism in the Holy Spirit". I was really clueless as to what this all meant.

The majority of the school were posh, and miles ahead of me in the amount of self-confidence they had, not to mention money. I assumed that I would never be able to speak out for God in the way that some of them did. They all seemed bigger, better, bolder and far more together than I was, as if they were of a different species. However, one kindly soul, an older girl from a big, fancy church in town, lent me a book to read by an American called Don Basham. I read it – or rather, inhaled it – and thereafter desperately wanted this gift of God, the infilling of the Holy Spirit. I prayed and did, of course, receive him, together with the gift of tongues. I resisted all attempts to dissuade me and by the end of the school year was accepted by a Bible college. I would be a missionary, and write and tend a big garden in my spare time. I would learn how to be really grown up and teach people Bible truths and be busy all day long with reading the Bible and praying. I would learn how to be strong and full of faith and God would be proud of me for being a good girl.

Chapter
4

A Challenge

The aerial on the battered TV set was wonky. "A bit like the whole of this place," said Phil. "It looks beaten up, but I bet it works just fine." The frayed and faded old curtains covered huge Victorian windows, and the book-lined walls and dusty-musty smell of years of reading and learning was enticing. My pastor, Philip Greenslade, and I sank into deep, large, old armchairs, sun slanting through the windows spotlighting the dancing dust, and waited drowsily to hear the result of my interview with the principal of this college, the Birmingham Bible Institute. Suddenly a tall, upright figure burst in, black robes flying. We jumped to our feet. "You're in. See you in October." He screwed up his face in a mischievous grin, turned on his heel and swept out.

Phil's eyes met mine as we stood up and stared blankly at each other, then erupted in delight, hugging each other as if I had just won the pools. On the way out I looked around at the threadbare carpet and the battered cars outside in the overgrown driveway and began to wonder what on earth I had done. What have I signed up for? Will I survive? Will I be good enough?

It was a crowded time, the three years I spent at BBI. Three brilliant, scary, challenging, glorious, exhilarating and over-whelming years. They were full of deep and intense discussions, raucous laughter, hours and hours of study, scary

ordeals of public speaking and preaching, exhausting and
tedious chores, and the most sincere times of worship I am
ever likely to participate in this side of heaven. And it was all
done together, as one. We were "church" all the time, 24/7.
We were also poor. Of the 120 students there, none of us had
much in the way of worldly goods. Even if we had come from
affluent backgrounds (and most hadn't), we all survived on
the same very basic diet, and lived and worked in the same
frugal conditions. Our food was less than exotic (we once had
potato pie and chips for dinner). Leftovers seemed to stretch
over many days, and watery soup and jam sandwiches figured largely on the menu. But of faith and good humour
there was plenty. We all ate together, prayed together, worked
together, argued together and grew together. We learnt to be
community.

And me? I was taking two diplomas at the same time, the
college's own one plus an extra-mural one from London
University, so I had no time to be complacent. The learning
part was exhilarating; a whole new world of faith possibilities
and biblical truth was opening up before me. I loved it all. My
mind eagerly scooped up the facts, the classes, the learning,
the reading. But the fight was now on in earnest – against the
crushing isolation I had begun to taste before I left home.
Somehow the more people were around me, the closer they
grew to me, the more apart from them I felt.

I was not like the others. I somehow didn't seem to live in
their world. My fellow students chatted excitedly together
from the start. I didn't know how to do that, what to say, how
to join in. They wandered in and out of each other's rooms; I
knocked on every door, even the common room, and waited
nervously to be invited in. I had no right to expect to be one
of them if I didn't think the way they did. They seemed to
know how to live, but for me it was an effort. I never did get

the hang of being awake and alert all day and sleeping all night. In fact nights were a series of waking and sleeping, activity and rest, and have been for most of my life. Others didn't get as tired as I did, or as anxious about things. I fretted about things that they took in their stride quite easily. I was apart. An "other". My journal at this time was littered with phrases like "wish I could contribute to the conversation"; "don't understand their reaction to me"; "feel I am keeping something back from them"; "felt lonely"; "hunger for real fellowship".

I interpreted my loneliness as simply that I was not walking closely enough with God, and rigorously tried to discipline my thoughts and actions into line with what I thought he wanted. But this seemed to serve only to isolate me further. I carefully watched the behaviour and actions of the other students, listening closely to what they talked about and how they related to each other, and tried to copy them. But I failed miserably. I just wasn't "normal" like them.

One day two girls shared with me that they felt I judged people, making them feel spiritually inferior. I was gutted – I was the one who felt inferior and had no idea I was passing on such things to them. I constantly, constantly asked God to cut me down, break me, mould me. I dearly wanted to be humble and penitent. I wouldn't attend some meetings because I felt that I might hinder the prayers. One evening in I wrote, "Wish I could come to an end of myself – I am weary of being selfish and proud. Oh that Christ would swallow me up in his love." I was so sincere that it hurt.

Going home for the holidays was an ordeal which seemed to get harder and harder. I dreaded each approaching term end and prayed for the ability to love my family. It never really happened though, not the love bit. Even in my home church the crushing loneliness made me feel miserable. I longed for someone to ask me out for coffee, or to chat, and was elated at every caring approach. I stood on the sidelines and watched church happen, but could never feel, it seemed, to be part of it. Just before Christmas I wrote in my journal: "Why do I crave love from other Christians? Isn't God's love in Jesus enough? It must be that my faith in Jesus is so weak that I need tangible evidence of his love and acceptance. I wish I could just accept being alone." A few days later I recorded, "Why do I worry about being rejected? It is when I take my eyes off Jesus. Foolish child! Will I never learn?" And, "Oh that I could, would, walk in the Spirit. Oh that I could minister Jesus by my every word and action. Surely the Spirit of God can do something with my feeble attempts at being a child of the Most High." And in January: "I just feel like a little worm, of no significance whatsoever, a complete and utter failure. But God has not cast me off."

It appears that the other students were as confused as I was with the person before them. The strange jumble of vulnerability and strength, timidity and confidence; the unpredictability of my actions and moods; the sense of not understanding nor being understood, set me apart from everyone else. I so longed to belong, and yet dared not intrude upon lives which seemed to be lived in a different world to mine. I felt I would spoil things for them, rock their boat, ruffle their feathers, be a spanner in the works. Then, I was sure, they would push me away – and I could not bear that. So I politely stayed on the fringe of others' lives, quietly visiting, briefly, when invited. One day I wrote, "Sometimes I wonder who I am", and another, "Have not yet found the real me". That, of course, was the whole point.

Meanwhile Bible college life rumbled on. The days were chock-full, the schedule beginning at 6.30 a.m. with prayers and ending at 10.15 p.m. when the doors were locked after the last prayer meetings, with lights out at 10.30 p.m. In between was the long round of lectures and chores. Not much chance to laze about in there. Even going to the loo sometimes meant risking being late for a lecture (and that was frowned upon). Weekends were no party either. Each Saturday we went out on evangelistic excursions – to the city centre, into the pubs, door to door, wherever there were people there we were. And on Sundays many of us visited churches to preach, sing or testify. A crash course in time management was lived out among us.

Among this pressure a less than humdrum situation was unfolding. One of the students, my room-mate in fact, in the first term of my second year, became ill. Actually, not physically ill but spiritually. It was said by those in authority that she was "demonized" and, for some reason I never figured out, she had to stay in bed. And so there she was, sometimes moaning and wailing in a very unnerving manner. It was my job as her roommate to fetch her meals and see to her needs – an exhausting task as we were in a little attic room under the eaves that was reached by a series of winding stairs, narrow passages and small doorways. These were old, romantic, fairy-tale buildings; I half expected to collide with the White Rabbit hurtling round a blind bend in a narrow passage! The doors of the many solid oak wardrobes in the bedrooms were just asking to be opened for a Lucy or Edmund to peer into the fur-coated depths of a Narnian winter. Great fun places to explore at leisure but the novelty wears thin when time is pressured. Dragging your own tired body up and down the steps with heavy trays loses its appeal really quickly, especially when the challenge of distant friendships and the inspiration of learning beckons elsewhere.

But, eager as ever to be of some use, I tackled this opportunity to prove myself with all the energy I could muster. As far as the real work of freeing my room-mate went, that was only for the holy and awesome staff to do, often leaving me sitting on the stairs outside waiting for the prayers and victory songs to end before I could enter my room. Sometimes it was late at night or the early hours of the morning, and the room was shrouded in shadows and mystery, before they let me go to bed.

It was on one such night that something happened which added significantly to my sense of isolation and differentness. The atmosphere of darkness and oppression in the little room was as thick as ever this particular night, the heavy black of evil was present and I shuddered as I got ready for bed. Jenny was sleeping restlessly, groaning and murmuring deep beneath the covers in the bed along the opposite wall to mine. I turned off the dim yellow lamp and climbed wearily into my bed, which faced the small casement window. Then I saw a silver-blue shadow slither around Jenny's bed, around the window and then disappear into the pane. I knew exactly what it was; it was the manifestation of an evil spirit. I knew that I knew but didn't know why I knew. I was not afraid, but rather, mystified. It was not the appearance of the shadow that bothered me; it was the familiarity of it that made me feel disturbed to my very core. It seemed that something within me was wakened, and I was deeply unhappy and very shaken.

What did I really see? Why was it so familiar? Had I seen these things somewhere before? What was that stirring of long-forgotten, far-away terror inside me? These things began an awareness not only of spiritual activity but also of my own mind. The faint echoes of distress that I knew haunted my mind took a more audible form – a crying child. She would be with me for a very long time to come, sometimes whimpering pathetically, sometimes screaming incessantly, always in a pleading, desperate way.

My feelings were becoming too deep, too raw, too unexplainable. It hurt even to contemplate the "why" of what was going on in me. All I could do was to hang on tightly to God. After that I stopped writing in my journal. My last entry for almost three years, 16 November 1974, was a quote from Daniel 6:26 – "For he is the living God and he endures for ever; his kingdom will not be destroyed, his dominion will never end. He rescues and he saves; he performs signs and wonders in the heavens and on the earth. He has rescued Daniel from the power of the lions." Then I wrote: "There are many lions around me today. God is going to bring me through the midst of them untouched. He has stopped their mouths, and put a wall of protection around me." I was, by now, exhausted, confused, trying to be brave but very, very lonely. It wasn't only Jenny who was experiencing oppression.

I was nineteen-years-old and becoming increasingly aware of spiritual activity, both good and bad, astonishing some of the students and staff by my knowledge. I really did see angels – the most awe-inspiring, scary and yet breathtakingly beautiful sight of tall, quiet, shining beings. I usually said nothing when I sensed or saw them when we were worshipping, or even when I saw something dark and demonic lurking around someone for whom we were praying. But very occasionally I shared a thought or awareness, but what seemed quite obvious to me appeared to be some mighty revelation to others. So I also was astonished – that others did not appear to know, believe or understand about spiritual things in the same way and to the same degree that I did. Of course there were demons. They are common, everywhere. I took that as a given. Why even discuss it? And doesn't everyone see angels when they worship?

This wasn't the only worrying thing haunting my mind. Friends at college who had tried to get close to me, to be helpful, told me I had a huge rejection issue to work through. I wasn't sure what that meant, and even less sure what to do about it, but it alarmed me that people were looking at me, peering into my life, into my soul. What might they discover? Surely having friends meant that they would allow me to minister to them, not that they had access to my secrets? More disturbing to me still was the question: I have nothing to hide… do I? I have always tried so hard to be a good girl. Everything's all right if you are a good girl, isn't it? The idea of examining my mind, my past, was too frightening to entertain.

In January 1975, after the first week back after the Christmas break, I was rushed into hospital, sirens blaring. I hadn't slept the entire week in spite of powerful sleeping tablets, and my heart was going so fast I thought I was going to die. The initial diagnosis was glandular fever, then emotional exhaustion, and I was later told in very serious tones that I had had a nervous breakdown. I spent the week in hospital crying pitifully and almost constantly, the sobs seemed to come from deep within my bones. I felt like a ball of black despair and failure, I just didn't know what to do any more. I didn't know how to live. I wasn't sure who to trust, who could help me, who would ever understand, or know, what it was like to be me.

But I must pull myself together, and fast. People must never know what was going on inside. They may think I was trying to get attention, or was being self-centred, and that is not what Jesus wants. He wants me to be self-sacrificing, give, give and give, so that's what I will do. I want to bless those around me not drag them down. Good girls aren't weak; I must laugh and be happy. I mustn't break down but be strong – nobody had told me (or had I just not heard?) that that was not the point at all. The point was that we don't have to try to be anything other than who we are; Jesus has done the "good" bit for us. So I made every effort to pull myself up by my emotional bootstraps. Above all else they must not ask questions, must not delve too deep. No one must know how bad I really am.

The real shock came when, in spite of my clear instructions to the hospital staff not to let them, my parents turned up to visit me. *No!* I did *not* want to see them. Suddenly I was fine. "There's really nothing wrong with me, thanks. You can go home now, Mum, I'm just a bit tired that's all. Been burning the candle at both ends, you know what students are like; yes, everything's fine; anything to get out of homiletics, eh! Thanks for coming anyway, probably be out tomorrow; bye then…"

"Phew! That was close – they had no right to be here. I don't want them looking into my life. Why didn't they stay at home?" I felt badly shaken that they came and saw my vulnerability; they must have noticed my blotchy face and red eyes. But they're my parents, other people seem to want to be with their parents, so why the anxiety? Why the anger at their taking the trouble to make the three-hour trip to visit me, their daughter, in hospital? What do I have to hide? Why don't I want them to know me, to know my pain?

I recovered enough to be discharged after a week but flatly refused to go home. In my panic I would have gone anywhere, *anywhere*, but there – it did not feel a safe place to be. I returned to college but no one, including me, could quite understand what was really wrong. Yes, the regime here was demanding with a fairly heavy academic workload plus practical chores and evangelism, but that did not faze me in the least. Study I could take in my stride, in fact I revelled in the rich discoveries I was making in my exploration of the Bible and the world of Christian thought and argument. The quality of the thorough teaching was excellent, and living in the college was not the problem. I was.

I loved the evangelistic challenge each weekend. The Saturday night pub work was thrilling and a rush of adrenaline was required to enter these shady, often dangerous establishments. But it was more than that. The knowledge that we were part of a huge divine plan to reach the hurting with the gospel gave us a buzz far outweighing any hardships: we were joining our efforts with countless saints throughout the ages! We went out armed only with a pocket full of tracts, a solid prayer backing and enough enthusiasm to topple the Berlin Wall. We triumphantly carried with us the sense that Almighty God was not only on our side but also had commissioned us to do this, and would tell us what to say, and to whom. What a task! What a privilege! And then to watch as amazing miracles took place before our eyes. Loud Irish jokers listening intently in a crowded bar to the gospel message, along with quiet Muslim men who picked up tracts in their native tongue, and half-drunk Englishmen who wanted us to sing songs remembered from Sunday school days. Sometimes they would allow us to pray for them. One thin, worn-out, ragged lady I spoke to longed to know forgiveness and salvation. She had lived a life of promiscuity and now, impoverished and alone, she wanted to pray. The only private place was the ladies lavatory, so we knelt to pray on the cold, damp stone floor out the back and together we wept. The walls were green with slime, the smell rank, but God came that night.

The rest of my stay at the college was an enormous challenge. I was faced not just with the study load, the Spartan living conditions, and the challenge of evangelism in sometimes-hostile conditions but also with the numbing effects of anti-depressant drugs. I had developed full-blown, black, menacing, clinical depression and various doctors felt they knew what was best for me. In the seventies these drugs were pretty basic and had unpleasant side effects such as a constantly dry mouth, constipation and the feeling of being in a zombie-like state. The tormenting thoughts that had begun soon after the Jenny incident had stepped up their pressure, and I was invaded by the incessant crying from a child in my head. The drugs had no effect on those whatsoever.

I developed a fear of eating, then full-blown anorexia. Somehow I felt that I should not do anything that felt as nice as eating – if only I were able to punish myself adequately for not being a good enough girl, then perhaps I would eventually feel that I deserved treats. But not now. Not yet. Eating lost its charm. Each meal was a challenge and guilt set in each time I tackled a meal. The feeling of fullness or gastronomic satisfaction was followed closely by regret so acute it was as if a white-hot branding iron had made its searing mark on my sensitive conscience. It would just be cooling when another meal would reinforce the immovable mark that said, "You are greedy. You don't deserve pleasure. You don't deserve to eat. You shouldn't have done that. You are bad. You should not have done that".

Insomnia was now chronic; with so much going on in my head during the day the nights were more tormenting than the days.

I did my best to study, and really enjoyed learning, but had a real problem with memory. Whole periods of time were a blur, if not unaccounted for altogether. But amazingly I passed both diplomas at the end of my time at college, one with distinction. That was a huge surprise; I hardly remember the exams at all. The only thing that stands out in my mind was the long train journey to London each day to sit the exams, and the feeling of being almost drunk with exhaustion by the time I got there. How I managed to write sometimes two three-hour papers a day over a couple of weeks was a mystery to me for a very long time. Until I understood.

But my longing to be "ordinary" grew to desperation point. How come I can't do and be the same as others? How come I found I have already done things I am just gearing up to do? How come I seem unable to form close relationships? How come I can't both sleep all night and stay awake all day? How come I seem unable to eat three meals a day without huge amounts of anxiety? Ordinary people do all those things without thinking. By the time I left BBI at 21 I felt old and anxious.

It seemed that when I grew close to the Lord bad things happened, almost without exception. When I interceded for others, I hurt deep inside and sometimes even vomited. It began to feel as though I was, or should be, evil. And the screaming in my head grew louder, the never-ending distressed cry of a very frightened child. I knew that she had been a good girl and yet it hadn't worked. I had been wrong: everything doesn't work out all right when you are good.

Chapter
5

A Choice

Somehow or other my attention was caught by a young man at college who appeared less threatening than most. He was not among the intellectuals I usually spent my time with, earnestly debating finer theological points. He didn't appear to dwell overmuch on the meaning of life. In fact he spent a great deal of time laughing, as I recall. I used to watch him across the crowded, buzzing dining room, enthralling his listeners with long-winded stories about nothing in particular. But his humour was infectious and the whole table would erupt as he roared at his own jokes. Tender-hearted, he often noticed those who were sitting alone or were not as popular as others, and that, above all, was what attracted me. He had, at the same time, noticed a certain young lady and the general college gossip, we later learned, was how best to bring John and Carrie together. A plan was hatched.

One day I walked into the common room and every overstuffed armchair was occupied, not by people, although there were a few lounging or reading, but by coats or books or bags. There was however, one free place, on a sofa next to another boy. Though slightly surprised at the amount of clutter around that day, I sat down on the empty seat without a second thought. The boy next to me happened to be John, and with red faces we chatted politely until it was time to get ready for evening lectures. Neither of us had noticed the exchanged glances and sly grins from the other students. Once outside in the hallway I put on my coat and was about to leave when the door swung open and out catapulted John. Suddenly. As one might who had been picked up and thrown headfirst. He came to land beside me rather ruffled and dishevelled but, as usual, laughing. He grinned his request to walk me back to my house. Though rather embarrassed, I shyly agreed.

John opened the side door and was immediately soaked by the torrent of rain lashing outside. He slammed the door shut and said, without a moment's hesitation, "You'd better jump on."

"What?" I asked.

"Jump on, jump on my back. It's tipping it down outside, you'll get soaked. It's ever so muddy." He bent over.

Too astonished to speak I unceremoniously scrambled onto his back, clutching my very full briefcase. Off we went together in the pouring rain – John galloping hard, head down, no coat, and I, hanging on tight, arms clasped clumsily round his neck, briefcase bumping wildly against his shoulder. Does this mean I now have a boyfriend?

Technically speaking I suppose that was our first shared experience, our first date, our first romantic encounter. That was to be the beginning of something beautiful, as they say, and also a relationship that has survived many, many unorthodox, unconventional and incredibly traumatising experiences. John always remained the same solid, steady, reliable man; seeing the joke in the darkness, the flower amid the rubbish.

I left college but the exhaustion and depression that had set in after the Jenny episodes followed me home. I found a job in a residential home for the elderly, but it lasted only four months before I was asked to leave. The long 45-hour week, the low pay, the heavy lifting with much running to and fro with meals and bedpans, and the demands of a stern and unreasonable matron resulted in a further collapse in my health. I just folded up under the strain in tears and exhaustion. Nevertheless I loved those old ladies, and they loved me. I know they did, they told me so. After a busy working Christmas the doctor ordered me to take a month off, and in response matron sternly felt this post was not for me. My feelings swung like a pair of old scales from feeling a complete failure to a solid certainty that God must have better things mapped out for me.

A troop of other jobs followed, each becoming more menial and each ending in exhaustion. Eventually the doctor signed me off indefinitely due to long-term depressive exhaustion. I clung onto the only real hope I knew, that God was in charge here and would somehow sort out the whole sorry mess that was my life. The inner crying continued, though I still was not aware that I was experiencing anything that others did not. That wretched child just kept on and on. She would not stop her pitiful screams and wails.

I spent a lot of time in the house alone, waiting nervously for someone to come. I would get up in the morning with great expectancy, clean the house when my parents had left for work, and sit and wait. Day after day after day. Who was I waiting for? I well remember the day it dawned on me that nobody was going to come. I needn't keep the house so pristine. It didn't matter if the cushions were not just so. Nobody would see them. Nobody cared. Why was I trying to impress people who never came, who never were going to come? And who were they anyway? What was going on? Who was I expecting? I couldn't relax, though; I felt I just had to be prepared and must not be caught off guard.

By this time Granny had died, and the aunties no longer came. Both my parents now worked during the day and my sister was also working. I felt foolish but even then, though I knew with my head that no one was coming, it did not penetrate to some other part of me. I continued to wait, anxious and tense, day in, day out, with all around me spotless. My hair was shining and my clothes immaculate. I would clear up the kitchen and wash up the dishes as soon as I had prepared a meal or even made a coffee – absolutely nothing must be out of place. It was very, very important that I do everything perfectly. It does not pay to get it wrong. I must be a good girl.

John and I wrote religiously to each other as he was still in college. His letters were so full of happy gossip, of ordinary life; he kept me grounded in reality. He was such a resilient character, full of laughs and buoyancy, able to take whatever came along with stoic acceptance. He didn't appear to be in the least fazed by my inner confusion, if he noticed it at all. We talked about anything and everything together, except my feelings – but that was not because I wanted to keep them from him, I just didn't have the self-awareness or the maturity to be able to articulate what was going on.

In due course, after a mail order courtship, John and I got married. It all happened on a shoestring, the ceremony taking place in my home church with the minimum of expenditure. We immediately moved up to the north, to John's hometown, and had a job waiting for us as youth workers with seven churches of different denominations. We lived in a little terraced house on the edge of the city, amid hundreds of other terraced houses, many of which were "back to back". Life was lived in community – our neighbours all knew us and we knew them during those "Coronation Street" days.

Life was busy and fruitful. Our lives were totally engulfed with the needs of the youngsters, aged eleven to eighteen, and our home was open to them. We worked during the week within each church, holding youth meetings almost every day of the week either after school or in the evenings. We also went into the local schools and spoke about the love of God and the exciting purpose he could bring into their lives. The school staff were all amazingly open to us and allowed us to speak in assemblies as well as Christian Union meetings.

Both John and I really loved those young people. They were, on the whole, "unchurched" and completely free from any religious hypocrisy. We took them on outings, had them over for meals, and were fully engaged in their lives. Their family backgrounds were often confusing, and sometimes we were not sure who was related to who, and their spontaneous and boisterous behaviour was totally unlike anything I had encountered in the suburban, polite, respectable south. The cheeky freshness of their approach to our message and us was both infuriating and delightful. We were constantly challenged.

Every Saturday night we had a crowd of youngsters in our home, meeting in the attic. Our phone was half way down the stairs, and when it rang we would have to dash down the carpet-less steps to answer it. These resourceful rascals found a way of making it ring when we were in the middle of the evening's message. One of us would hurtle down the stairs, only to find no one at the other end. It took us a few weeks to figure out what was going on! Of course, the youngsters enjoyed that immensely! The joke was well and truly on us.

We headed a small team who joined us in our goal of bringing the message of Christ to these kids, and it was their support, enthusiasm and joy that kept us going in the difficult times. Pat, Maurice, Judith and Trevor were our buddies and our backbone. We grew and groaned together at the daunting prospect of facing forty or fifty yelling, over-active and rebellious teens each Saturday night. We screamed at them, prayed for them and loved them. Over 200 commitments to Christ were made during those turbulent and exciting few years.

Many youngsters grew and matured in the Lord; some are now in full-time Christian ministry. A new move of God was ushered in while we were there, channelled by John Wimber and the Vineyard teams. We found ourselves right in the middle of exciting events as the Holy Spirit swept through the church and the city. Every-member ministry was emerging, and John and I were among those who not only got to attend the dynamic conferences, but also entertained the Vineyard teams in our home. We saw others being released from bondage through our ministry. "And great grace was upon them all" (Acts 4:33).

But not, it appeared, on me. On the outside I had, with my husband, a growing ministry as part of a thriving, charismatic church. We understood how to wait and watch for the Spirit's move in someone's life. After a couple of years as paid youth workers, John had to look for a secular job as the churches could not afford to continue to fund us – we had accomplished what they had asked and each church now had a thriving youth work. It was a wrench for us both and it was with sadness but characteristic stoicism that John turned his attention to looking for another job. He had already been a part-time driver for a sweet company and drove round the Yorkshire countryside in a brightly painted van to supplement our income. But he had to find a full-time job now, so he began working as a clerical officer for the DHSS. As I was more available than John – we decided together that I would stay at home to continue our work in the church – I was called upon many times to minister to people, often in depth, sometimes taking many hours, and was later even on the deliverance team. I could "do the stuff" as it said on our T-shirts. Helping others was the easy part. Helping myself – I didn't know how.

The wholeness around me didn't touch me, not the deep parts of me that were hurting so badly. I sometimes wondered if I were two people. One was the successful minister; the other the crying, lonely child. Or perhaps even more than two, for I also felt I was very, very evil. And somehow there were also bossy, noisy or aggressive parts too. I felt a dark, creeping sensation when I worshipped in the Spirit, or did anything in the Spirit, and it was increasingly disturbing. Sometimes I thought I might be going mad. Insomnia was a chronic problem and when I did sleep it would be disturbed and I would wake with night visions – being covered in ants or strangled by snakes. One memorable night I awoke to find a semi-naked, painted Zulu-type warrior beside me, spear in hand ready to strike me. It went but I was unnerved, confused. I struggled not just with black depression but the voices in my head told me I was getting it wrong, I couldn't do anything right. I was bad, evil, and should not be in church, in ministry. The constant criticism meant that I tried even harder to be the perfect Christian. I so wanted to love and to serve, and tried to do so with all my might.

As we were no longer working with the young people, opportunities opened up for a ministry to alcoholics, and later with travellers, as we led evening "welcome groups" for enquirers and young Christians. I also led a group for young housewives, many of whom were suffering from depression. But the sobbing, the internal distress, increasingly intruded on anything I sought to do for others. In spite of John's caring and stable presence and our fulfilling and challenging lives, it felt as though I was standing alone in a vast and empty arena, with no one to come for me. I was completely unable to express to John at that time any of what I felt. In fact I felt guilty for not being completely happy – weren't we now doing all that we had longed to do when we prayed and planned together during our college days?

It was as if I was hiding a collection of abandoned children who had no one to comfort them. Who would dress their wounds or clothe their pathetic naked little bodies. Where, indeed, was my comfort? God was doing amazing things for those around me, but why wasn't he healing me? And what do I want him to heal me of? Why do I hurt so badly? Haven't I always been a good girl?

At one Vineyard conference, when the Holy Spirit was invited to come upon the hundreds present, a loud wail pierced the air with great volume and urgency. It was several moments before I realized that the horrible sound was actually coming from my own mouth. My whole being seemed to be in immense pain and I could no more prevent the sound from coming than speak Swahili. I knew that God was present and I also knew a gut-wrenching conflict inside. John and friends, with me at the time, could only look on in confusion and helplessness while I fought my inner battles alone.

I really am not aware, still, what happened then. There are vague images in my mind of being on the floor with a crowd of people around me, praying. They were looking at me – me, in the humiliating position of being curled up in a ball or shouting or crying. I hated it all. There were other meetings on other days when something similar happened and I would come to, not aware of what really took place. I know that I was often taken out into a small room and that I sometimes ran out of the door, and sometimes physically wrestled with them. Always I was left feeling drained, embarrassed and confused. But I was assured that I was OK and that God was doing something mighty. But what, exactly? And why wasn't it all over now?

I returned home but my weight fell by half a stone – everything I tried to eat tasted like wet sand. It felt as though the anorexia was returning; it wasn't that I chose not to eat in order to punish myself, this time I just did not want to eat. I was hurriedly, worriedly sent by the church elders to a healing centre in the north to receive "deliverance" prayer. The people there explained to me that I must have received some early trauma that involved something satanic and that I was "demonized". God could do something about that and I was to submit to him. I was instructed to lie down on a blanket placed specifically for the purpose, and the four people ministering to me sat on my two outstretched arms, on my feet and one straddled my body. They shouted at the demons and fought with me as I struggled to free myself. They tried to be very loving and caring and sought not to traumatize me further. They failed. The whole experience was hugely disturbing. I ended up in shock. I don't remember much after they "anointed" my navel with oil and then poured wine down my throat as I screamed. The event lasted hours and when eventually it ended I ran out of the building and down the mile-long drive to the main road as fast as I could.

I have since come to understand that although Christians in ministry may have the very best of intentions they, like everybody, sometimes get it wrong. They "got it wrong" that day in their assumptions that my distress and violent reactions were caused simply by oppressive demonic presence. I was to learn so much more in the months and years ahead about these "manifestations" and the awful secrets contained in them.

I shared very little of these struggles with anybody, and certainly kept mum about the crying child in my head. When I told a gentle, sensitive elder what kind of things were going on inside my mind I was quietly led away for prayer. There were further deliverances, and I began to wonder if I must have thousands of demons, because my response to their prayers was so dramatic. I wrote in my journal in January 1986:

Apparently I have been delivered of lots of demons, well over a dozen. If that is really true, then hadn't I ought to be rejoicing on cloud nine, rather than taking anti-depressants (drugs)? Could I possibly have been oppressed by such a number of evil spirits and yet still be functioning, though in a limited way I admit, in the power of the Holy Spirit? And if those times of ministry weren't actual deliverance, what *was* going on? Was I making it all up – an ego trip into the spiritual realm? An attention-seeking ploy? A sign of dementia or madness? These latter thoughts fill me with disgust and abhorrence more than that of being indwelt by something evil. My heart in all good conscience says that it was outside of my control, those times of reaction when prayer was made for me. It was like suddenly being someone else. I feel as if I would like to tell someone about it all... what it feels like to find yourself crying out or fighting or using foul language and yet have no control or even any inclination of what will happen next. It's like being under an anaesthetic, or just going unconscious, when the world outside is like a dream.

There was always a big fight, with struggles and screams. I felt completely powerless to do anything about it all. Then I would stop, exhausted, and everyone would rejoice that now I was free. Only – I wasn't.

All the prayers and ministry had no positive effect as far as the depression, the voices and the incessant talking in my head went. It wasn't until some time later that I would fully understand what was really happening. Antidepressants only served to make me feel drowsy and slow. What on earth was wrong with me? I must be evil after all. In fact I increasingly had the feeling that I should not be, should never have been, a Christian: "I can't do this. It is wrong for me. I only mess things up for everyone else. I am a liability. And it is altogether too hard. It is easier for me to not try to resist the enemy, but to give in and be done with it." Twice that actually happened. Weeks later I recalled them in my journal:

The depths to which I had sunk don't bear thinking about, but his [Satan's] pull was so strong, and the battle had been so hard, so long that in my folly and weakness I gave in. Both those occasions took place in the night, and both times his [Satan's] presence was very real and I was very tired. The last time I felt so dirty and so far from God that I felt that I couldn't possibly ever be acceptable to him again. He is holiness and purity and the vileness and repulsiveness and dirt of my life through my contact with Satan made me feel that even to sing about God would physically hurt me. I felt sick and heavy all the next day. It was the Sunday before Christmas and even being with God's people was an uncomfortable experience. I didn't belong with them; the purity was too bright for me. During the carol service I decided that I would have to leave the church and forget about being a Christian. Keith [an elder] had told me earlier in the day that a decision had to be made, would I follow God or the devil. By 7pm that night my mind was made up. I couldn't continue with God – it was too hard; I was too weak; the temptations to sin, to swear, to provoke, to think immoral things, to hurt and destroy were too great for me. I was tired of trying to resist a constant onslaught of temptations like these from outside myself not within – I could never have thought such things. Never.

Someone took the trouble to spend some time with me, and I returned to the Lord. But times like this only served to shake any confidence in myself that was left. I was in a battle and I knew it. It was a battle for my life but it all took place in my mind. That's where it all happened. In spite of it all God kept me from falling. I wrote:

Satan can take everything away from me; he can prevent material prosperity from coming; he can make me unpopular or a nuisance... he can disturb me, weaken me, taunt me, tempt me and take me so low that I feel as though I'm in hell. But he cannot destroy me. He would try to destroy my home, my marriage, my health, my peace, but he could never, ever succeed in destroying my soul, and ultimately he would never be allowed to destroy any of these other things either. Thank you Jesus.

On the outside things were tough too. By now we had two small children to care for – Amy, at just three years old, was a bubbly, inquisitive little girl and Luke a very content baby. I was delighted to have them, having been told from the start that I may not be able to have children, and if I did it would be by Caesarean section. But amazingly I had two natural births. I loved them to bits, but the daily task of looking after them was incredibly daunting; much of the time I wanted to be the child rather than the parent. We had only John's meagre income to live on.

It was not all bad. Our financial challenges had a way of teasing out our creativity. For example, one day five-year-old Amy was home from school with chickenpox, little Luke was fed up with playing indoors, John was under pressure at work and the heavy November days were grey with cold and rain. I decided it was time for a celebration. But what to celebrate? The children and I set to work making party hats and goody bags ready for our tea-time party. When John arrived home from work we all gathered around the festive table, complete with jelly for dessert. I had decided – we would have a "chickenpox party"! Luke was thrilled to be wearing the silly hats we had made and we sang "Happy chickenpox to you" to Amy who blew out the candles on the cake with great enthusiasm. Then came the party games. It cheered us all up – we had each other and so much besides.

There were other good family memories too. Lots of them. Like winter picnics on the sitting-room floor, outings on the bus to the local hills, and at Christmas the flurry of present making. We would sometimes skip down the street together, all holding hands so that we straddled the whole pavement, laughing all the time. Luke's little legs could barely touch the ground!

It was the eighties, but we had neither a car nor a television, a freezer, microwave nor automatic washing machine, so our life was more full of lengthy domestic chores than many of our friends', and occasionally I felt ripped off, though I struggled hard to look for God in everything. The truth was, one income was simply not enough. I was far too weary after a day of childcare and ministry to others to think of doing an evening cleaning job – the only available option. But the financial strain was dire. I wanted to live "victoriously" but found that very hard. On 5 February I wrote: "I have decided to take the absolute minimum of money from John and trust God for our food. Today I helped with the ministers' meeting at lunch time, and came back with enough food to help out for the next two days. If that is the beginning, with little faith, I'm sure that as my faith grows so will our provision."

Two weeks later I recorded:

Am feeling depressed today... there is so much to do and no money to do it with. There isn't even enough to adequately feed us all. Helen gave me some washing powder today... but the feeling of having to scrape about once again for well-balanced meals over the weekend and next week makes my heart sink so low... am very tired. My heart is heavy and so are my eyelids. The ironing tonight took one hour forty minutes, and I've by no means finished. There's a pile of wet washing to be dried. The children were tired and grisly today... Sometimes my life feels so insignificant, wish I had a goal to aim at, though suppose loving Jesus is enough. I want him to do with me what he wills with this boring, wasted, messed-up life of mine. I do wish right now there was someone to hug. Father is showing me my pride – how I hate it! How much purifying needs to be done in me! Why do I grumble at my lot? My Lord and God has to cut out the dead wood, train my hands for war and my feet for standing firm. Keep your chin up Bramhall, and hope in him!

I decided that I needed more discipline in my life, for if I really was a good girl then things might be easier:

> Am becoming increasingly aware of my need for more discipline in my life. For what purpose? To make more room for God and in so doing bring order and the proper placing of priorities in my life. Unless I can hear God in the circumstances of everyday living my life is being wrongly directed, time is being wasted and I end up drifting through each day.

Although we were both involved in leading groups of various kinds in church, we were feeling the call of God to move on. Our two children were growing up fast, and if we wanted to make any moves it would mean a great upheaval for them to move once they were both settled in school. We had been getting itchy feet as far as ministry was concerned. After lots of soul-searching, prayer and some amazing words and works of God, we made the decision to accept the invitation of our American friends in the Vineyard, and move to California. This was not a decision we made lightly but we had always both shared a hankering for full-time ministry and knew that this opportunity was from God. It has to be said, however, that I was, from the start, the driving force behind it all. John was naturally far more cautious, and I felt that I was leading, no, tugging him. Once we had begun to seriously consider this move the idea of leaving the country felt so freeing for me, I just could not wait to go. It felt as if this was what I had been yearning for all along, so this is what we had to do, and we had to do it *now*.

After that things happened astonishingly fast. The house was put on the market and sold within a few weeks. The money for our airfare was given to us. We gave our possessions away at an alarming rate and the things we wanted to keep we sent over to the States. Left with very little, our clothes and a few essentials, the children having to play with toys I made out of cardboard boxes, we spent our last couple of months in England saying our goodbyes. We stayed for a few weeks with some friends who lived nearby.

We were slightly anxious about what we would do when we first reached the States, because our shipped-out things would not arrive until several weeks after we did. We prayed about it and left it with God. One day I received a phone call at our friends'. A very apologetic voice on the other end of the phone said, "I am so sorry Mrs Bramhall, but it appears a mistake has been made. This is the first time anything like this has happened in our removals company. But the container with your goods in has left before the appointed time, by some fluke we cannot explain, and will be there some time before we originally said. This seems to be the one that got away!" As it happened our furniture arrived in San Francisco before we did and there was no awkward waiting time! We knew that had to be the Lord. He had cared for us tenderly from the very beginning, and we were sure that we were in the palm of his hand.

What we didn't know of course was what lay ahead. If we had known of the trauma and seismic eruptions that were to blow our lives apart in the next few years, the excitement and hope which buoyed us up would have been replaced by rather darker emotions.

Part 2

Chapter
6

Disturbance

The sun is astonishingly warm in California even in January. The sky is permanently a deep blue colour and the strong sunlight brightens every colour. The space is amazing – so much of it! Lots and lots of unfilled air where your eyes can span spacious miles. As we drove into Fresno, rows of cotton plants or vines stretched long into the hazy distance; line upon line of regimented orange and peach trees, each standing in a puddle of hose water, stretched to the edge of the world. I felt drunk with space. I wanted to run with outstretched arms and feel the soft spring breeze on my face; the high sun warm on my cheek. Space to breathe and grow. "I like it here. Yes, I like it here."

It felt safer here in California. Away from high grey stone buildings and heavy rain; from suffocating traffic and tense conversation; from sad, stressed people and runny-nosed children. Here, large cars lumbered leisurely along wide roads without hurry or worry and everything seemed slower and quieter.

The occasional puff of wind is gentle and kind, unlike the Yorkshire gales that leave you nowhere to hide. The stillness, the brightness captivated me from the moment I touched Californian soil. Here, in Fresno, California, is where I had longed to be without realizing it. I could leave behind the depression and the dark, sucking vortex of inner pain. I could now forget about the night terrors and make a fresh start. No more snakes and demons. What a fool I had been to imagine crying babies and nagging voices in my head. Now I could start to be a real person. How could anyone feel unhappy in this holiday land?

But things turned out difficult from the start. First of all, the promised job and home never materialized. Whether it was a figment of someone's imagination all along or whether something just went wrong I never knew. But we ended up with no home of our own, no job and all four of us squeezed into someone's tiny spare room, sharing one sofa-bed between us and feeling surplus to requirements.

The hardest part of those first few weeks was seeing John so distressed. He was normally such a resilient man who consistently bounced back; but this time he was not bouncing – he was crying. He actually longed for the wind and the rain and the grey struggle. Without those things he lost his fight and emotionally crumbled in the ease and pointlessness of sunny, carefree, laid-back California. I was shocked, horrified – I had never seen him cry before. I felt responsible and guilty. I felt I had dragged him away from his home and all that he knew and loved. It was all my fault. I had taken our darling children from all that was safe and familiar, and all because some unnamed fear haunted me so much that I felt I had to get out. The children were confused and bewildered. They no longer had a home or a sense of belonging. Carolyn – what have you done? Everything was going pear-shaped; it was not supposed to be like this.

Just a week after we arrived I wrote in my journal:

We are strangers in a foreign land. We are different. Unfamiliar. Not part of anyone's lives. Our experience of life is not like theirs. Divided by a common language we are misunderstood and we misunderstand. We have no home of our own, no job, no means of transport, no school for the children, and hardest of all, no church. What's going on, Lord?... They [Americans] have so much – large houses... large cars... but we know far more about cramped homes, weary housewives, leisure starvation, unemployment, boredom and the despair of poverty. What are we doing here? The poor among the rich, commissioned to feed the hungry and clothe the naked?

It seemed absurd. What on earth was God doing?

Of course, things change, they always do. Within weeks we were opening a home for abused women. A local doctor had a facility he wanted to make available to the distressed or disadvantaged and felt that we were just the ones to start some kind of refuge there – perhaps for abused women? So we found a home to rent for ourselves, took up his challenge, and began to build our lives again. Our bright little Amy, was eventually settled in a school that suited her to some degree – it was hard for her as she was way ahead of others of her age. The school starting age was six in California and she, now six herself, had been in school for two years and could read and write quite well. In fact during those early days of settling in she was reading the Narnia Chronicles by C.S. Lewis, while her classmates were still learning their ABCs. But she made valiant attempts to make friends and, after some time of upheaval and false starts settled down in a class above her age group. Four-year-old Luke went to preschool several days a week and, though a little shy, soon played happily with his new chums. We began to allow ourselves to relax into the new culture. We had no money behind us but were asked by the board of the home to run it "by faith". So that's what we did.

Soon a wonderfully resourceful woman called Dorothy

joined us, and she proved to be a real gem. One day the three of us were praying in "Agape", the refuge-to-be, preparing for the official opening in a few weeks' time. We were asking the Lord for the $200 we needed to repair the air conditioning. A knock came at the door and Dorothy went to answer it while we went on praying. She returned with a cheque in her hand for $200! Someone we had never met had felt it right to come and give it to us. Nobody knew we were there – as it was to be a safe place we did not give out our location – nor did anyone know we needed that money!

One Saturday, when the home was up and running, we had almost run out of toilet rolls. In the evening we left our band of loyal and dedicated volunteers in charge so that we could have a rare Sunday off and go to church, but wondered how they would manage in that department until our next money gift came in. We said nothing to anyone but simply prayed. After the service the next morning, a lady rather sheepishly approached me with a large black plastic bag. In apologetic tones she wondered whether we needed any of these? Inside the bag were dozens of toilet rolls!

Sometimes we were paid and sometimes not – we still were not able to legally receive a wage, but it was agreed that we would be given a gratuity when it was there. For the most part we had to pray in our basic needs. Late one Friday evening, John had already gone to bed; I was tired but very aware that our cupboards were almost empty. Just a tin or two of sweet corn (people always gave us that!) and some pasta. I was clutched by a whim to write out a full shopping list as if I had money like any normal housewife. I brashly wrote out my wish list including extras like fun biscuits for the children, our favourite cheeses and a rare treat – meat. Totally exhausted after a long day at the refuge I had no energy left for ardent prayer, so I waved the list in the air and went to bed.

The next morning John, forever the reliable and stable daddy, took the children for their usual Saturday morning visit to the library while I stared blankly at the tins of sweet corn thinking of lunch. Just then Maggie, one of our valued volunteers, called by and told me she had just been to the hairdresser, also a Christian. "That's nice," I said. Apparently that kind lady had heard of our work in "Agape" and wanted to contribute, so had gone shopping with us in mind. Maggie went back to her car and returned, followed by her two teenage children and her husband, each with arms laden with brown paper bags. They set them down on the kitchen table, exchanged a few pleasantries, and left.

I emptied the groceries onto the table. Incredibly, everything that was on my shopping list from the night before was there, including fancy biscuits for the children and some real meat. Well actually no, not quite everything. There was no cheese. Impulsively I said out loud, "Lord, you've forgotten the cheese!", chuckled to myself and cheerfully put everything away in our bare cupboards. I later went out to empty our mailbox. Inside I found an envelope containing an anonymous note and a cheque. The Lord said to me, "You get to choose your cheese!"

Our little refuge thrived and we were always full. Though it housed only seven women at a time we also tried to provide food and clothing to those who were not able to stay. With twenty-four hour supervision necessary it was hard work in the heat of a desert town like Madera. Many of our residents were Hispanic and spoke very little English, and we also had rape victims or unwanted pregnancies to deal with. Some women were hiding from abusive partners, many were illegal aliens from Mexico, all were in desperate straits. There were challenges on all fronts, and we felt inadequate and totally cast upon the Lord. To gather some tools to aid us I enrolled in a Crisis Pregnancy Counselling course down in Fresno, thirty miles away.

It was gut wrenching. They showed video clips and gave information which was deeply disturbing and my head began to spin out of control. Something bad was happening. Something inside was being awakened. I felt alarmed and panicky and didn't know how to handle it, didn't know what to do. There was a petite, smiley, gentle lady in charge, called Shirley; should I talk to her? What would I say? I bottled out for fear of making a nuisance of myself. But by the third day I collapsed – I just "went away" somehow and came round on the floor surrounded by paramedics and firefighters. They all acted so busy and officious, flapping and jostling, asking me questions I couldn't answer. I was rushed to hospital in the ambulance. It all happened so fast, before my mind could make sense of it all. They admitted me to the psych. ward – they had noticed some nasty wounds on my arm that I could not explain. I was so embarrassed I wanted to curl up and die. "Stop! I'm English! I'm respectable! I don't do mental wards!"

I could hear the other patients calling or crying from their rooms, and lay in stunned despair as I struggled to come to terms with my new identity as a mental patient. My eyes ached from crying, and just when I thought there couldn't possibly be any tears left the weeping started again. Where's God? The awareness that I was locked away brought waves of shame and embarrassment and a fresh flow of tears. Within a few days I was moved upstairs to the less acute ward where I met others who, like myself, were burned out or depressed rather than psychotic. At least these people seemed more ordinary, but never in a million years would I have imagined being a patient in such a place. This was not supposed to happen; this is not OK. This is my new, happy life in California. I should not be in a mental ward. I'm OK really. Honest.

Ward 7 West treated me kindly enough, but I did not respond well to the group therapy sessions. I didn't know what to say. I seemed to give the wrong answers, in fact the doctors didn't appear to believe me, they wanted me to say something else. I didn't understand. And I seemed to be getting worse. I would faint or "check out" at the least provocation, like being asked about my childhood or my family, and would go away to another part of my mind. The slightest thing seemed to knock out my ability to stay in the present, and then I would fall unconscious to the floor. I was walking on eggshells, not knowing quite what would trigger another collapse. If I didn't know what to say in response to a question the words in my mind would shoot off into space, leaving a blank, and then I would "go away". When I returned I would feel foolish and embarrassed. Staff members were clear that there was no physical reason for my faints. I must be faking it; I must be a fraud. I was horrified.

Some of them were sympathetic, others suspicious; some were angry and tried to bully me into stopping the "game". One day I wanted to be alone, so went along to the balcony overlooking the city. It was caged, presumably to stop people like me from flinging themselves off. It was good to breathe the fresh November air through the steel wire, to see the deep blue expanse of sky, to hear the sounds of traffic and everyday life seven floors below. I tried to get my mind straight – what was going on? If only the crying would stop. That stupid child…she shouldn't be in my head anyway… Wish she'd fling herself off this balcony, perhaps then I'd get some peace. Something once again switched off in my head and I was gone. I "came to" some time later lying on the concrete floor but still in the same place. No one was about. I had fallen on my glasses and bent the frames. Apart from a few bruises I realized I was OK and tottered back to my room.

It was time to stop hiding in the blank that were my emotions. I knew I had to start talking about my feelings but was not at all sure where to begin or what to say. Suppose I say the wrong thing. I am English. We are not taught, as our American friends are, how to put feelings into words, but I did my best. I didn't see many visitors, and that was all right with me as I was too tired and too ashamed to feel comfortable with others. But I also felt embarrassed about my apparent unpopularity, because it became known that I was a Christian. I thought it reflected badly on the church that I seemed not to be really cared about much. If I were, then wouldn't people come to see me? Am I an embarrassment?

My only visitor was John. Poor John – left to carry the can. Two children to care for, a refuge to run, volunteers to oversee, distressed women to deal with, food, donations, clothing… So much on his shoulders. How could you, Carolyn? How *could* you?

His visits had been full of difficulty – I felt so guilty that I was not being the wife and mother the family needed and deserved. He was being such a brick, carrying on being a great dad as well as running the home. But he began to seriously wonder if we should have come here at all. I felt panicked by these doubts, we mustn't even think of returning. I couldn't blame them, it wasn't their fault I was messed up inside. But John's presence reminded me painfully of England, and that triggered more repulsion and anger than I had room for.

So I didn't even want to see him, couldn't see him. His confused, kind face triggered something too painful to deal with, so I rejected his visits, and was alone. It was my choice; I chose to push John away, though he made such valiant efforts to continue to visit for a while. Soon even his endurance came to an end, and admitting defeat, though in grief and confusion, he turned his attention to the children and the work and left me to wander in my own wilderness.

But Shirley, the manager for the Crisis Pregnancy course came, sometimes early in the morning before work, sometimes when she had finished for the day. I suppose the problems started when I began to depend upon her short, cheerful visits. She made me feel wanted and special, her affection and attention became a lifeline to me. So I substituted Shirley for John as my main source of comfort. That, of course, was a big mistake. John was hurt and confused and I knew it, but out of a sense of desperation I continued to resist the pull of my shredded conscience, trying to push away the awareness that I was hurting the three people I loved most in all the world. Even that love could not overcome the sense that I was fighting for something else, something that threatened my survival.

Shirley and her husband, Matt, came one day in early December to take me to church and then out for Sunday lunch. I was nervous but pleased, grateful for their love. As the service was starting Shirley and I smiled at each other. I put my hand on her knee as a gesture of affection, but when her smile faded I quickly took it away, thinking no more of it. After the service we went to the back room for a special time of prayer Shirley had arranged for me. I had high hopes that God would really do something for me that day. But somehow, somewhere things went wrong. Shirley didn't speak to me at all, the prayer was hurried through and I was hustled away. When we reached the car she told me we were not going out to dinner, she and Matt had decided it would be best if they took me straight back to the hospital. They gave no explanation, and coldly ignored my questions and angry tears. I could sense her displeasure and I felt hurt and confused. What had I done wrong? She seemed the most important person in the world to me but was clearly offended with me. Just before saying goodbye she told me that she probably would not be seeing me again. My fragile world collapsed.

For the next few days I cried constantly. I didn't want to eat, and couldn't sleep. I spent hours in the hospital chapel asking God, "Why?" Have I been bad? I always try to be a good girl, but I must have really blown it this time. Shirley doesn't like me any more; I am not a nice person. Why can't I just be good and then things would go well with me, and people would like me, and I would be happy. Life is so very hard.

I was still coming to terms with Shirley's sudden exit when I received another bombshell – I was to leave hospital in two days' time. The insurance money had run out. Well or not, I would have to leave.

That prospect was frightening. It was safe and secure on the ward; I knew what was expected of me, and on the whole did not have to pretend much. Now I would have to play the together, happy Christian, the normal wife and mother, but something dark was going on in my head and there would be nowhere to run to for refuge. What would happen if I checked out in front of my family or friends? I wouldn't be able to explain it. I couldn't just carry on; there was nothing left in me to give.

However, the day I returned home was scarily wonderful. John and the children were deliriously happy to have me home again. In our large, airy lounge stood a huge Christmas tree, heavy with decorations and presents, given by our wonderfully generous friends, Vivian and David. We were loved after all, as a family, as a unit. That included me. It was time I stopped messing about and got on with the job of being the best wife and mother I could be.

It was good to feel "grown up" again and resume the role of wife to a down-to-earth, practical husband. John didn't deal in feelings or talk in psychological jargon. He thought about routines and shopping and buying petrol. He was full of news of the volunteers and the nitty gritty, nuts and bolts of daily living, and I loved him for it. I had forgotten how much I loved to feel Amy and Luke's warm little snugly bodies, to hear them prattling excitedly away about their adventures, to enjoy their unquestioning dependence. Both of them were readily affectionate and I was more than eager to reassure them of my love and offer my attention. I have always enjoyed being creative with the little we have, and the challenge of making life fun and stimulating for my two little imps pushed me to reach for all the possibilities life offers. I even enjoyed clothing them with cast-off garments so that they looked really good and felt special. I swung back over to being the capable mum.

My children were a delight. Luke was the mischievous one, forever plotting another trick to play on Dad, while Amy, the bookworm, was full of questions. She always, always needed an adequate explanation for the wonders of the world, and had an uncanny way of knowing when she was not given the full story. It was good to be back on board the family ship, and back in the galley too, planning the meals and fitting into the routine again.

But I wasn't secure in that role. Something had changed. It felt that I was filling in time until something else happened, something inevitable, something bad. That sense of foreboding preoccupying my mind only heightened the crying, frantic child in my head. My life seemed to be on hold, as part of me was elsewhere, ready to go, and on full alert. A deep loneliness moved in, as I felt disconnected from those around me. One journal entry in December went: "O God, O God, rescue me from the depths of confusion and deception and loneliness" and the following day: "Felt almost suicidal this morning... Feel low and unconnected with anyone, kind of cut off even from the people who love me."

Later that month I met with a Dr Christopher Rosik, a psychologist who had been recommended to me. He worked at a care centre primarily ministering to returning missionaries, called Link Care. After the appointment I wrote that I felt "increasingly depressed, lethargic, tired and uncomfortable. Don't know what to do, don't know what to do – how do I make it go away? Wish someone was here to hug me very tight – but no, if they did I would love them too much and they'd go away and I'd feel abandoned and alone."

What was to become of me? Of us? Was I good enough to carry on living?

Chapter
7

Decline

Our work at "Agape" had to end; it was clear I could not cope with its demands.

That left us high and dry, as the work permit still had not come. With no job how could we expect to receive anything from anywhere? Then the gifts started coming in: a bike for Amy, a train set for Luke, a cheque from our church in England. John had a free haircut, then another cheque arrived, food from another friend, another box of goodies, food stamps – all within a few weeks. To crown it nicely at the end of the month I passed my driving test. But the dark cloud continued to hover menacingly around me.

I continued in therapy with Christopher, paying for it by cleaning houses, churches, anything that would earn the necessary funding – I was desperate to continue in this exploration of my past. I was also still occasionally blanking out. One day I had an unexpected and disturbing image in my mind of a large man's buttocks right in my face. It felt like the memory of a time when I was really small. In my journal I wrote: "I felt panicky and horrid and unclean and bad and scared and confused." Other images or memories came: "of being held down and a vision of large muscular, bare arms around me. Then the awful feeling of confusion because I was naked – that cannot be right – but then it must be OK because grown-ups are there."

3 April: "Whatever happened as a child has left me with a thousand screams of fear."

I had occasionally cut myself in order to see the pain on the outside and somehow assure myself that I was a real person.

6 April: "My arm is still smarting and I hope it continues. I want it to hurt because on the inside it hurts."

Other disturbing things were emerging, flowing out uninvited; memories that had been locked away. I spoke them out to Christopher who accepted it all without judgment or intrusion. He didn't probe, but was there for me, to listen and reassure.

More journal entries from April:

I remember the green sofa. There was at least one woman in the room. And men. I should have had clothes on. I shouldn't be here. They shouldn't be laughing. Are they laughing at me? My feet are cold. Please can I go now? There's a white cloth, square, soft with fraying edges. Warm like winter sheets. Why is it on my face, it means I can't see? I can't see. It's hard to breathe. Why do they laugh? I can't breathe. Am I allowed to struggle? Let me go, I want to go now. It hurts. They mustn't hurt me... NO, NO, NO, NO, NO.

The screams continue. There's something inside my head that's dark and foreboding, a kind of terror.

In May we gratefully received $450 in gifts from different people to help out as my parents came over to stay with us for a holiday. Of course they must come. They love us and miss us. While they were with us I cut myself again. This time eighteen slashes, with lots of blood. I managed to hide it from everyone, even from John, and was becoming quite expert at presenting a happy front and then phoning Link Care late at night to release all the pent-up anxiety.

By June I was beginning to regress to a child state in therapy. We had been in the States eighteen months. At the same time life went on in the world outside of my head. We continued to be blessed with gifts of money and provision. John helped out with a Native American friend's church in Madera, the children were happy in their schools, and I had submitted some of my writing to publishers. I had won the "Golden Poet of the Year Award" for a poem about Amy, two others had been published and an article about burnout had been accepted by *Decision* Magazine, the highly acclaimed magazine of the Billy Graham Association, which had the largest readership in the world for a Christian periodical. It was never published. I was asked to make a few simple alterations but I didn't ever follow through – I was unable to believe they really wanted it. I continued to write and submit poems for publication, and some were accepted. But the financial gains were small.

The Lord continued to provide for our needs as we searched for voluntary Christian work opportunities while waiting for our visa. A job came along in the beautiful Sierra Nevada Mountains just east of Fresno. So off we went. Just getting there was an adventure. Before we even left Fresno a kitchen chair fell off along the freeway and we had to stop to tie it back on. Our humble belongings were carted precariously up the steep, winding roads to the ranch on the side of a mountain in a ramshackle truck driven by our Native American pastor friend. We followed the truck in our battered Pontiac, packed to the gunnels and coughing and struggling valiantly. But then on a remote mountain road we ran over a small boulder and had a puncture. Stranded and praying, we waited. Eventually an ex Los Angeles police officer appeared from nowhere and put us back on the road.

The Sierra Nevada Mountains are beautiful. I had always

wanted to live in a place which had pine trees and mountains, just like in the story of "Heidi". The ranch, which was
to be our workplace and home, nestled in a small dip, where
a lake provided cool water for the many deer that roamed the
forest. The ranch dog was part wolf, part Alsatian, and often
accompanied me to the quiet, leafy haven I had found for
myself among the forest undergrowth. There was a pony and
rattlesnakes, deep snow in the winter, the call of birds and at
night eerie, echoey, unfamiliar sounds. And then there were
the trees. Mile upon mile of huge Sequoia giants, reaching to
the sky, standing with their feet dug deep in the dry, brown
debris of branches and bracken littering the forest floor. These
evergreen monsters that whispered and swayed in tune to the
seasons were my shy friends and confidants.

Our stay in the mountains lasted just nine months but felt
like nine years. We lived in an unfinished, unfurnished house
next door to the ranch for teenagers who needed private care
and schooling, having been rescued from the Southern
Californian drug and beach culture. These kids had it all
materially but knew little about love and nurture. We worked
every day with them in the schoolroom above our downstairs
flat. John, with infinite patience, guided the youngsters
through the home-schooling programme and I taught the
corporate lessons of art and music. Not that I had had any
experience – I just taught the way I wished I had been taught
these things. We had a lot of fun. John really revelled in this
work and showed skills neither of us was aware he had. While
I loved the mountains, life was more an endurance test of
coping with the everyday, while feeling preoccupied with the
underlying stuff of therapy.

Once a week I travelled the fifty miles down into Fresno to
see Christopher, often staying overnight, and then returning
laden with food, gifts, library books – whatever could be

found that was free or cheap. I wanted to bring the children treats to cheer them up, to reassure them that Mummy still loved them with all her heart, and did not go away because of them. I wanted to try to give them what other children had. Amy and Luke looked forward to their weekly pile of library books to devour and a gaudy paper bag full of goodies Mummy had found: an orange, a toy from the dollar store, some candy (they came free at most banks), colouring sheets and crayons (free from restaurants), a book from the thrift store. Sometimes friends in Fresno would bless us with clothes for the children too, or something good to eat. We both worked hard but could not legally receive a wage, so we shared meals at the ranch and trusted God for petrol and everything else. Sometimes we had to be creative with the things that came our way. One day a whole truckload of muffins was donated to the ranch, which was also run as a Christian charity and so trusted God to provide. We were eating muffins for months – for breakfast, lunch and dinner; with cheese, with jam, with salad; hot, cold and indifferent. What could possibly be done with a muffin, we did! Another time it was melons.

It was hard being so far from "safe" people. The conflict of being two people inside increased – one the capable, creative, fun teacher, wife and mum; the other the terrified child remembering horrors of the past; the snivelling victim, desperately searching for something she feels no hope of finding. Hopeless despair living side by side with nurturing optimism. But it looked as if we would have to give up any hope of expecting to obtain a work permit, and without that we could not stay.

On one point I was certain – I would not, could not, return to England. Everything in me shouted "No". The heaviness of the prospect of having to leave California and return to England was crushing. I was at last beginning to feel that I was in a safe place because I could speak openly about my pain to someone. Christopher was a professional so would be less likely to cut and run when things got demanding. I just could not give up that place of shelter just as things were getting unbearable on the inside. And England seemed increasingly dangerous, as if I had just escaped from threat and impending disaster of the worst kind. I wrote in my journal that I struggled to cope with "the crying child in my mind constantly begging not to be taken where she does not want to go". And I had started to pass out again.

I was living on the brink. This must be what the Puritans called "the soul's winter-time". But I was just too barren and cold to bear it. To continue to live like this seemed pure torture, and the alternative appeared quite attractive, sometimes almost inevitable. One day I had decided quite definitely that I could not carry on living. I sat in Maggie's study where she let me sleep when I was staying in Fresno overnight, and wrote my last notes to those I loved:

Dearest John

I'm sorry I have to do this to you, I know how much you love me. You have been so patient, and I love you for it. Thank you for sticking by me. Thank you for being an excellent father to our children. Thank you for allowing me the space to grow and make mistakes.

Please give yourself permission to start again; I want you to find someone else to be the Bramhall wife and mother. You are young and attractive. My darling, my heart is sad to leave you, for a time, but I cannot bear any more pain. I am engulfed in darkness, and for too long the light and beauty has been so distant. I can't wait any longer for it to move closer. I need to be home with my Father.

I will always love you,

Your own

Carolyn

Darling Luke

I am proud of you, my Big Boy! How clever you are to ride your bike, and you do such lovely drawings... Mama is very tired and has to go home to be with Jesus, but I will see you again, in heaven, so you must ask him to be your very special friend. Your Mama has had to hold on very tightly to Jesus' hand when I've been afraid. When you feel lonely and sad when I've gone, I want you to do that too.

Daddy loves you very much, he will look after you well. Be good for me, my darling little boy.

I will always love you

Mama

Darling Amy

You are my special little girl, and I love you so much. I have to go home to be with Jesus now, but you will see me again in heaven. I am so proud of you, one day you will make people very happy with your writing – that's what Mummy wanted to do but I am too tired to do it now.

I know you will be very sad when I have gone, but know that it is not because you were bad or naughty, because you're not. I go because I want you to have people around you who can love you even better than I can.

Daddy loves you very much and will take good care of you. I love you, Flossy. Be good for me, and keep on looking at the beautiful things around you.

Your loving

Mummy

Dear Christopher

You have played a very special part in my life these last seven months and I will always be grateful to our God that he placed you there. Thank you for all your patience and encouragements, the extra time and concern has not gone unnoticed...

Now that I am going I can dare to say I am proud to have

known you, and I don't want you to think that you have, in any
way, failed me. You succeeded in making a lot of darkness bearable, and a lot of heaviness lighter.

Thank you a million times. May the Father continue to build
that solid and sure knowledge of his presence in your life.
With gratitude and love
Carolyn

I had it all sussed in my mind. But, once again, God had
other plans. A life-saving phone call to Christopher helped
me to see things in a different way. We talked long and hard,
and my resolve to take my own life was broken. Perhaps there
is hope after all. But I kept the notes anyway, just in case.
Dying was always an option, a way out of the excruciating
inner pain that was almost a physical feeling in my stomach.
I ached for something I didn't have, had never had, but so
desperately needed. I knew with my mind that Jesus could
give it to me, but somehow I couldn't connect with that.

Life was tough in every way. Bills came and we had no
money to pay them. Our second Christmas in the States was
approaching and there seemed no prospect of buying presents for the children or having the funds to send my hand-
made presents home to England. The house needed attention
– we're not talking luxuries here but walls and doors. We survived the very cold, snowy winter without a proper outside
wall on one side of the house, just a large piece of board
between us and the snow. It was our bedroom wall and we
could feel the penetrating cold coming through the board at
night. There was no dividing wall between the living room
and our bedroom either; we hung a curtain, Heath-Robinson
style, to provide us with some privacy. The young people had
to pass through the flat to go upstairs to the schoolroom, and
in the evenings that meant walking through the children's

bedroom while they were in bed. Not an ideal situation, but Amy and Luke never once complained. Neither did John; and I was so glad to be in America and not in England so serious grumbling was not on the agenda, though things were far from ideal. But we struggled to understand when the main ranch house next door had attractive alterations made while we still needed the basics.

On the other hand, we were blessed. God never left us without hope and people who loved us in his name. Maggie invited us to stay for Christmas, and so Christmas Day was spent in the warmth and comfort of her lovely home down in the valley. There were presents for the children, and for a brief time we could enjoy being together, with enough to eat, away from the pressures of the ranch, and put to one side the harsh realities of our precarious situation.

In therapy it became clear that I had been abused, but also that something in another realm, something sinister and very frightening, had happened. When I was remembering things I would "dissociate" – which means I would split away from my self, and click into another mode of being. In passing from one state of consciousness to another I often toppled over, thus the "blanking out" episodes earlier. At least I now had a word for what had been happening in me for so long. I would act in an uncharacteristically child-like way, detailing things that could only be described as overtly evil, even satanic. Christopher took me to see a friend of his called Doug who ran a Christian home for ex-addicts. He offered deliverance prayer, speaking against the evil beings that were influencing me, and commanding them to leave. Although Christopher was a very professional and, in some ways, conventional psychologist, he recognized the importance of taking into account a client's spiritual experiences. He knew that the Bible speaks of evil in a personified way, and even though he would not profess to understand it all he was willing to admit that the fight between good and evil played a very significant part in the human struggle.

The experience at Doug's was both frightening and enlightening. I began to describe evil and demonic entities in a detailed way, completely consistent, I was later to learn, with what is known of ancient demons. I described, in my child-state, things I called "the Black", "the Green" and "the Orange" among others. I even drew pictures of what they looked like, though afterwards I didn't remember doing it.

Working hard in the ranch kitchen or schoolroom felt unreal. What felt real was "the creeping, black realization that something cruel, unfair and awful happened to me a long time ago, and it is still alive inside of me… Living is a heavy burden."

I wrote to Christopher:

Jesus came for people like me, didn't he, Chris?… And God is the greatest psychologist, isn't he? It seems to me there is no hope except through him… Over and over again a tape is playing in my head – something awful has happened, something awful has happened, something awful has happened. I don't want to believe it. It's like a searing pain; it wrenches me away from every security I had. I wish it hadn't happened. I *so* wish it hadn't happened… But it's time to put into practice all the theory about God I've been speaking of over the last twenty years.

It was becoming clear that we were verging on some dreadful revelation of my past. Could I bear what was about to emerge? On top of that it was looking unpromisingly as though we were officially illegal aliens, as still the work permit had not come. The director of the ranch was supposed to be applying for the permit on our behalf, but his heart was obviously not in it (he was having marriage problems, and then he and his wife divorced and the whole venture folded). He had missed the deadline for the application and things were looking dire. We had to think seriously about our future.

This did, of course, lead to the inevitable conclusion that we return to the UK. I was panicking. "No. I *won't* do that, I *can't* do that. No, *no*, NO." I was frantic. "I have just begun to trust somebody. It feels safe here. It is not safe in England. I cannot go. I will not go. *No.*"

I had an apparently unreasonable fear of returning. I felt as though I had done something really, really bad and would be "found out" if I returned to England. I could not understand myself – things were getting frighteningly out of hand. In my journal I wrote: "It's a dark place. It is too dangerous for me to be in England. I would have to *go*, in England. I would have to die. I couldn't just be. I would be too afraid."

What on earth was I talking about? I didn't know. I didn't understand myself. Who was I? I felt as though I was facing sure and certain doom.

"Maybe I'm not allowed to be happy," I wrote. "I want to be loved, I want to be loved, I want to be loved." Another day: "Why am I afraid of being seen? Why do I want to hide the fact of my existence?"

When things came to a head next door at the ranch, we were given thirty days' notice to leave. John made the decision – we are going back to England! Of course that is the most sensible thing to do. Of course he would come to that conclusion. Poor John, he never did settle in this laid-back, take-it-or-leave-it culture. But it was not like that for me. Time to panic! No, *no*, NO!

We had to make some firm decisions about our future, if only for the children's sake. So we talked: John would return to England with Amy and Luke, I would finish therapy with Christopher. In a couple of months, when I had got over these strange ideas, I would rejoin them and we'd build a new life together in England. It would be tough, we had lost almost everything materially, but we could always start again; we had each other, we had the knowledge that God is for us – who, or what, can be against us?

Chapter
8

Departure

As I prepared to face life alone another explosion occurred. Christopher gave me the diagnosis he had been contemplating for some time: Multiple Personality Disorder. That means that I am not just "me" but "us" – my personality had fragmented as a small child because of the way I was treated.

What happens is that when a child feels overwhelmed at the trauma occurring in her life, she would pretend that it wasn't really happening to her – it must be happening to somebody else. My daddy, or whoever, would not do things like that to me. He must be doing it to somebody who likes it (or deserves it, or can handle it). The little child would "go away" in her mind, and perhaps watch from a distance or from a "cloud", or maybe go right away into a safe world of her own creation. Another part of her would come out into the real world to take the abuse or trauma. That is what "dissociation" is all about – a separating of the self from reality. Painful memories are still all there, in the one mind, but the mind itself divides into segments in order to protect her sanity and enable her to carry on a somewhat normal life, completely amnesic to the harmful events.

That would explain some of the big mysteries in my life, why I often didn't remember all that went on in therapy, why I seemed to have conflicting emotions building and building for no reason, why I wrote things I didn't understand. Then came Christopher's other conclusion: I had been for some time describing satanic ritual abuse. I had been "chosen" to be the innocent, pure victim – mercifully, my twin sister had escaped that dubious "honour". What a help to discover that there was a name given to the events I saw – others had also experienced such things, I was not alone. That would explain my absolute terror of returning to England; the fear of being "found out" and in danger. It would also explain the presence of what seemed to be evil entities around and within me.

Initially I didn't want to believe him. But my anger gradually subsided and things began to make sense. It appears that traumatic memories are stored in a different part of the brain from those of normal, everyday events. So retrieving those kinds of memories would feel different, perhaps even as though they are not memories at all. It felt, for me, as though the things I was "seeing" in my head were things that happened to someone else, not to me. They seemed to be alien pictures, things I did not want to see, things I would not want to be associated with, things so sick and full of terror and darkness that they horrified me. It was as though I was remembering a half-forgotten horror movie, a vague reel of film playing out in my head that evoked deep and disturbing feelings.

Once the diagnosis was made things moved pretty fast. The child that "came out" such a lot with Christopher had a name: "JuJu". I would effectively switch out of being who I normally am, the adult, and become a different person in all kinds of ways – my facial expressions changed, the way I walked, talked, held my head and sat were different. I used different words, and put emphases on words in a different way. My eyes became much wider and my eyebrows seemed to perch higher on my forehead. I appeared to turn into a completely different person.

I was not aware at the time of the following details. Most have been gleaned from my journal entries, video and audiotapes of the therapy sessions and Christopher's notes. Only later was I to reclaim the memories of these events, as became stronger and more whole. I did have a small measure of "co-consciousness" where I was able to "watch" what was happening to and through me. It was rather like the experience of dreaming, or watching a television screen that was distant and faint. Afterwards I could sometimes recall events the way you remember a film you watched years before.

JuJu told Christopher that she was five years old and wore red dungarees; that she wasn't "all that very good" at tying up her long brown hair (mine was short) so it was a bit messy; and that her job inside of my head was to remember some of the bad things so that I didn't have to know. But when we got to talking about the past she seemed to be terrified of saying the wrong things and being punished for it. When she came out there was immediately a sense of tension; she stammered and stuttered in her struggle to explain the terrifying fears she had. She was very anxious, and jumped at the slightest unusual noise or what could be perceived as disapproval from Christopher. But she quickly learnt to trust him and would, unlike any other part in those early days, hold his hand when she felt insecure. She was capable of real warmth, too. She was, in fact, just like any very frightened five-year-old.

There were other parts too (Christopher called them "alters" or "alternate personalities") who revealed themselves at the beginning of this extraordinary journey. One was called "Janey". She was a "fussy little person" I recorded in my journal, "always moving, touching everything, trying doors, moving knobs, peering through cracks. She wants to play and explore and is more interested in things and how they work than people."

Another, "JC", at fourteen, was "strong, almost powerful in her presentation – with a good sense of responsibility. Anger is her predominant emotion, but she also has a solid sense of justice and her emotions run deep." "Carrie" was "the fragile china tea-cup one, easily offended, feeling unworthy, dirty and stupid. Her feelings of uncleanness spill over into all her actions and attitudes, resulting in a withdrawal from crowds, and socially demanding situations." We later discovered that Carrie was anorexic and many times stopped me eating; she had been made to eat things that were disgusting and vile, and understandably was not happy at the thought of anything in her mouth.

I also had a two-year-old alter, a boy called "Little Joey". Apparently his real name is Jonathan, which is also the name of the high priest who was in charge of the group I was taken to as a child. He was a personalization of the sacrificed children I saw in those horrific rituals that were playing through my mind like an unwanted horror movie. Bad dreams were becoming a regular occurrence and now, with the prospect of saying goodbye to John and the children, things felt altogether too much. I was overwhelmed and tried to run in every direction at once.

The dreadful day came and our belongings were packed up ready to be shipped back to England. John, Amy and Luke had said their goodbyes to friends, and we spent a couple of days exploring San Francisco as one last treat together before our parting. I sat and looked at my sleeping children as they lay together in the large bed in our bargain hotel room. Their cheeks were flushed and rosy, they looked so innocent and vulnerable. They desperately needed a mummy, but I was choosing to let them travel to live 6,000 miles away from me. I could hardly bear to think of life without them. And dear John – now suddenly head of a one-parent family, all because of my silly ideas. How would he cope? He was not usually the one who made the decisions in our house, he preferred to wait for me to make the first move, and then support me in it. What would he do when he had to decide whether or not to take them to the doctor, when he needed to talk to their schoolteacher, how to discipline them for being cheeky, even when to cut their toe-nails? I had learnt how to stretch a tight budget; he would not have had the benefit of that experience. "How will he manage?" I fretted, "Will he remember to stroke Luke's cheek the way he likes it when he is drifting off to sleep? Will he be firm with him about brushing his teeth? Will he know when Amy is grumpy because she is hungry and when it is because she is tired? And what about her lovely long hair – who will brush it till it shines and tie it in plaits that make her look so lovely? They need their mummy, and she won't be there."

They went and I was left behind. I will forever remember the look of bewilderment on Luke's face as he turned to wave at the departure gate at San Francisco Airport. No excited smile, only a questioning stare, brimming eyes wide as he watched his mummy disappear among the crowd. I watched in numb nothingness as the ones I loved most in all the world vanished behind the barriers. My beautiful children, my patient, loving husband. What had I done to them? What's to become of us, of me? I turned and made for the rest rooms and, in privacy and solitude, allowed my heart to break.

We wrote often to each other, of course. I so much appreciated John's strength and willingness to care for the children alone. I wrote to him soon after they left: "I am so proud of you – taking such a bold and courageous step in bringing the children back to England alone. I love you for it, and am confident that you can do a good job of bringing them up without me for a time... You are strong, my darling. I am indeed privileged to have such a patient, understanding and courageous husband... ".

Days later I was in fighting mood:

Hey! I know what's going on. It isn't God at all who is taking everything from me. It is Satan. He cannot kill my body so he is trying to kill my spirit. I no longer have a country, a family, a church, any money or very many possessions. I have no job, no profession and even my friends are backing away. But he cannot keep me down. I *will not* feel sorry for myself. I *will not* engage in a pity party. I *will not* slowly and quietly die on the inside so that I am no longer a threat to him. I will not only be a child of God, but I will be seen and heard to be one too. *So there, Satan!*

But avoiding pain is really painful. Your guilt sits heavily on the tender spots and the resulting aches pale the rest of life a deathly grey. Even a hint of joy is fragile and sore to touch. This whole inner system that had developed in order to keep me from knowing and feeling the truth was now breaking down. It had served its purpose; I had been blissfully ignorant of all that had happened when I was a child. Now things were falling apart, and so was I. In avoiding the reality all these years I had stored up a huge amount of un-dealt-with pain, and now it hurt terribly.

"I will try to be good," JuJu whimpered. "I will try to be good. Are you going to hurt me?... I will be still, I promise. I will be quiet. I will be still. I will be good." She popped out so often, usually unannounced, that I am never quite prepared for her, and neither is anyone else. A feeling of panic would begin deep in my gut and rise until I could no longer hold on. I would have to close my eyes to shut out the roaring, frantic terror, sometimes falling over sideways at the same time, then suddenly all would be quiet inside. I had switched out of that traumatic space. All of a sudden my eyes would open wide and out would peer an indomitably curious JuJu, insatiably hungry for reassurance, fearful (for now she held all of that roaring terror, not me) yet courageous.

At first it felt really bizarre, and I felt foolish when I returned – why is a sane thirty-something behaving like a very anxious five-year-old? What's to become of me? I wondered. I will be abandoned and forsaken, for how would anybody be able to handle who I am?

But there were some amazing people around who did understand. Heide was one of those.

I often visited Heide and her husband Edmundo; in fact I was to live with them in their little apartment for a while later on. Heide met and grew to know and love many of my alters, and they, especially JuJu, loved her. One day when JuJu was "out" she took her to ToysRUs and bought her a baby doll. I could only watch from a great distance. We named her Maisie. Dressed in a little blue and red gingham dress Maisie has been her comfort and companion through many difficult memories. I still have Maisie.

Heide later wrote to me about that time:

> There were times I was scared for what else you would find out about your life. I believed everything that you discovered about yourself because you were always honest and truthful. I surely did not understand how such horrible things could be done to any human being, but I believed them because of my own suffering and my own history.
>
> I fell totally in love with JuJu, who to me was the real you when little: scared, inquisitive, obedient, wanting to please and that's why I asked you if I could take her to the stores to look at books and toys. I wanted her to see at least what a little girl could see and feel like. Thank you for that experience, I will never forget it.
>
> This is just a little of what I felt, treasure, and will never forget!

God brought Heide into my life several months before, and she was an angel. I was low. Very low. The best thing for everyone, I felt, would be for me to die. Having "others" on the inside was bad enough, but when they began to describe evil things, overwhelming feelings followed and I wanted out.

It was late, I was down in Fresno for my weekly visit and I

parked outside Link Care to try and absorb some of the safety that seemed to ooze from that place. It was the most secure place in the world for me, though today it was dark and deserted. I sat and contemplated my next move. Yes, I would take all the tablets I had – they would be enough to send me into everlasting oblivion. I could walk down the road to the restaurant to buy a drink to wash them down, go back to the car and nobody would find me until the morning. By then I would be in heaven.

On the other hand, I wondered if the God I had believed in all these years could find another way out for me? I couldn't believe this was "it". Where was the abundant life Jesus spoke of? "I know what. I'll give him the chance to prove that he is real and has something better for me. I know this is crazy, but if someone were to come along and talk to me, late at night, on this empty cul-de-sac on the edge of a missionary campus, then I'll give life another chance. If no one comes within half an hour I will go and buy that drink. End it all. Decently. Without bothering anybody." John and the children? I could not bear to think of them. My pain wouldn't allow that agony of burden to enter the equation.

Minutes passed. I was not expecting anyone to come. It was really black; not even any street lamps. Even if someone were to come, they'd be in a car, I was in mine, why would they think to get out and speak to me? Time ticked by. Then a car wound slowly up the road to where I was parked. It would probably drive into the residents' car park. No, it stopped just near me, in the middle of the road. A passenger got out, walked over and knocked on my window. "Are you OK?" As I wound down the window I saw a round, smiling face, concern in her eyes, and I burst into tears. I followed her to her apartment and had a hot drink. My whole story poured out, and she listened intently, with genuine care.

And God said to me, "Carolyn, I really, really love you."

Chapter
9

Distressed

With John and the children gone I had to find a home, and went to stay once again with Pat and Don, who had opened their home to us when we first arrived in California. Now I didn't have responsibilities I felt freer to talk to Christopher about what I was remembering; it ceased to be freaky, and became just a normal part of my life.

Seven-year-old alter, Janey, came one day to describe one of the events she experienced. Janey was created to take the sexual abuse, but found using words difficult, preferring to act things out using dolls or perhaps just feel the difficult feelings. I was increasingly both horrified and sceptical about these memories – I had no recall of these things at all, though I couldn't imagine why I'd want to make it all up either. It felt as though it had all happened to somebody else, I was not there – it wasn't me – when those people did nasty things.

But then, *of course*, it didn't feel like me, that's the whole point of dissociation – to create distance between the victim and her experience of abuse. The alters were created for just that purpose: so that I'd not be aware that it happened to me, but rather to "others". The trouble is, in reality it was my body that took the abuse. It was only my mind that was divided, and sooner or later the amnesic barriers were bound to come down.

And that's exactly what had begun to happen as I heard

their stories. They triggered a vague and growing sense in me that this really *is* my story. I began to experience feelings so overwhelming that I didn't know what to do or where to go. Feelings of being trapped, of wanting, more than anything else in the world, to *get out*. Feelings of utter panic, as though I was running round in circles. The panic told me I had to do something, anything, to escape, but I didn't know what from. I would sometimes literally walk round and round, or be so agitated that I couldn't sit still or stop moving my hands or my feet.

Christopher had suggested we video some of the sessions to help me come to terms with my other selves as I had little recollection of them afterwards. One videoed session in particular was disturbing:

JuJu climbed the steep stairs. She was cold all over, they had taken her clothes off before she started the climb and the ancient, winding stone steps were rough and freezing on her bare feet. She reached the top with a man following closely behind her, but she didn't know what she was supposed to do next – and panicked, "I don't know what to do, I don't know what to do." Then she felt a large hand on her bottom and immediately she went away inside and Janey came out. Janey knew how to handle this sort of experience more than the other alters, for that was why she was created. She instinctively moved away and the man playfully said he was going to chase her. Janey ran round the small, dim, cold, musty-smelling room, from one corner to the next, with the man closely following her, laughing. The dust on the floor got between her toes and stuck to the soles of her feet. She was giggling as he caught her at last, and pushed her harshly against the wall, her little chest and tummy pressed hard against the cruel stone, her face turned sideways so that she could breathe. Her giggles were more like gasps now, as she was acutely aware of where the man's fingers were probing. The game had stopped, no one was laughing any more. This is what they do to her – Janey felt no emotion but accepted her lot: it's all she knew.

JuJu came to help her out, so the next thing Janey knew she was in another room, up a further flight of narrow steps. She was lying on a table and a bright light was focused on her. On the wall to her left the old wooden shutters to a small, deep window were closed tight, and in the corner opposite was a green, wooden cupboard pressed hard against the wall, with a small key still in the lock. There were other grown-ups there. They were tying her ankles with thin ropes that hung from the ceiling. The men and women who had gathered solemnly and soundlessly surrounded her and someone hoisted her legs into the air uncomfortably apart. She couldn't see much, not even her feet, as her head had been pulled backwards over the edge of the table.

She endured the next minutes, hours. She knew she had to be as still as she could, and not make a sound. That would mean she was good. The men and women who surrounded her solemnly and clinically had their way. Inside, "Beth" was staring, eyes wide, unblinking. She knew what was happening to the body; her job was to take all the despair that engulfed her in waves. As far as the inside people were concerned she was a pretty six-year-old, with blonde curls and wearing a frilly dress. She wasn't feeling pretty just now, but when it is all over she will retire to her soft blue room filled with cushions, in the depths of my psyche, and find some comfort. Beth's role was to feel the mental anguish and torment of these events when the black misery descended. At only six she could not understand why these things should happen to us. She is shy and easily upset; suspicious of most adults. She expects pain but is a sensitive child and longs to feel good inside. However, she likes little girl things – dainty dresses (unlike JuJu who is more comfortable in her red dungarees) and delights in pretty things. Beth was there at the back of most of the abuse events, struggling to come to terms with the "why" of it all, taking the overwhelming feelings, especially with the realization that some of those taking part were members of my own family.

As time wore on Janey went back inside because the pain was more than she could handle. At first she alternated with "Annie" who later took over from her completely to take the heaves of nausea, the numbing cold and the piercing, searing pain in her groin. Annie had thick, pale brown, untidy hair, slightly longer than shoulder length, which hung over her pale, drawn face. Her unkempt appearance was because she was in constant pain and bore the lethargy that comes with it. When Annie first started to come out and speak to Christopher she was so weak she was unable to sit up for very long. As she and others told their stories and the pressures on the inside were released, she gained strength. She slept a lot, and was largely unaware of things outside of the inner world. Annie alone handled physical pain and often stayed until it was all over.

JuJu, who was in and out constantly, was aware of most of what was happening, and held all the fear and terror of that night. She tried so hard to be good, believing that if she were they wouldn't hurt her so much. Before they left a man whispered in her ear. He would put frogs in her mouth if she wasn't good, he told her. She knew what he meant – she must never, ever tell. Sometimes she had been told that if she were good the knife that was put into her body openings wouldn't draw blood, but usually it did. She could never manage to be good enough.

JuJu stayed out as they pushed the table, with her still on

it, cold and sore, against the wall next to the green cupboard. She dare not make a sound or move a muscle. The adults all went; at last she was alone. On the outside all was dark and still but inside a lot was going on. Beth was quietly suffering the despair that comes with knowing people you loved had chosen to hurt you (for we recognized some of the faces); Janey was numb and shut down; Annie suffered from the continuing pain from the rough treatment and was shaking uncontrollably, and JC, full of anger, was fuming. On the outside JuJu calmed down as the darkness deepened. Eventually Polly, the depressed one, when all danger of any of the abusers returning was passed, came out to take her place. She lay alone in the cold and the dark, and cried.

Christopher sat quietly through to the end of the memory, constantly, quietly reassuring us that we were "remembering, just remembering. It isn't happening now. That all happened a long time ago. I am here. You can stop whenever you want to." But none of the alters wanted to stop until it was all told, every last detail. We wanted somebody to know.

Twice a week we visited Link Care, and sat in a bare little room with only a sofa (for me) and the dolls (for the child alters) and a chair (for Christopher). I needed no other stimulation, as my own mind was so full. There were so many, many things to tell. There were to be more events, more stories. Bit by sorry bit much of it came out over the following months in the bare but restful little room at Link Care, with Christopher making it safe.

When all the telling was over for the time being JuJu came out, but was still unsure of whether it was then or now.

"I will be good, I will be good, I will be good," she cried out in high-pitched terror.

Christopher quietly tried to explain: "You were a good girl, JuJu. The hurting had nothing to do with you. They hurt you because *they* were bad. They did some bad things to you that had nothing to do with you. You were trying to be as good as you could and you were more than good enough... they wanted to hurt you and it had nothing to do with you. You were a good girl, and did the best you could in a desperate situation. They intended to hurt you. But you did fine. They hurt you because they wanted to. Do you understand that?" JuJu nodded, but was not so sure. It didn't feel like that to her. As far as she was concerned she must have been so bad they had hurt her – her mind was made up on that one.

At the end of the session Christopher gently invited the alters to go back inside so that I could come back. I had been able to watch much, but not all, of this from the "inside". I was in shock.

"Will I ever forget?"

"No, I don't think you will," replied Christopher, "but it is like a cut that has healed but still has some dirt in there, so it hurts to touch. You have to go back in and clean it up. Then it can heal without leaving any pain. After that there's still a scar, but it doesn't hurt so much. Therapy is like going in and cleaning up the wound. The scar will always be there, but it won't hurt so much."

Quite often, after Janey had done her remembering, I would need to go to the bathroom and vomit. Sickened and shaken, a deep sense of repulsion and horror held me in an iron fist of unbelief and confusion.

I watched that video with a mixture of embarrassment, incredulity and relief. Janey used the dolls she had brought to act out the sordid details. When she had finished with those she lay on the floor and acted out the feelings. I was horrified to see her writhing and groaning her way through the parts of the event in which she was "out" and involved. JuJu, when she came out, was full of panic and fear but JC, having got over the injustice of it, was amazingly calm and relaxed about it all. They were each so different. Is this really me? Could I be making it up? Deep down the events they described resonated and echoed throughout my mind and body with foreboding familiarity. Like trying to remember a dream, but not quite catching the pictures, just the sobre atmosphere, the sour flavour, the malevolent mood. It all smelt of over-whelming darkness in every sense, the heaviness of fear, dis-tant voices, faces, sensations, all of them Bad. Very Bad.

There were an awful lot of inner wounds to clean up. Wounds that had to be reopened and allowed to bleed freely, just as Christopher had described. I was hurting more than I ever thought it was possible without dying of grief and inner agony. A mind-blowing and agonizing spear was stabbing at me: "They hurt you. These people hurt you. They took off your clothes. They laughed. They touched you. They did hor-rible things to you. Why did they do that? What had I done wrong? Why had I been so bad? I tried. I tried to be good and I wasn't good enough. Stupid girl."

The number of alters was becoming ridiculous. By mid-1990 I was embarrassed to discover that I could identify twenty-two alters, all of whom could be described in detail. For each alter had a look, a personality and preferences of his/her own. Sometimes their names told something of their appearance or character: "Whisper", "Bumble Bee", "Stormie", "The Searcher", "Jewels", "Old Nell" or "Pieces". It was as though a whole community inhabited me. Most of the alters were children and I grew to understand how they func-tioned on the inside. Once I had accepted their presence I could distinguish between them when they wanted to express themselves. Sometimes there were internal arguments and I would get a headache from all the bickering. There was one alter, strangely named "Honesty", who was determined to try to convince me, and Christopher, that all this was "rubbish" and I was imagining it. But then, if I were making it all up, I would be making her up too! She would scream at Christopher, "It never happened. Nothing ever happened. No! Nothing happened. You are stupid to believe it. It is all a load of stories. Nothing happened." She even wrote in my journal in her distinctive topsy-turvy handwriting, so different from mine. She was desperate to prevent me from finding out the truth; in fact they all felt that the truth would kill me. They were wrong. The truth gave me back my life. It is the truth that sets us free.

Things were difficult on the outside too. I was missing John and the children terribly. I heard regularly from John but it was the children's letters that were heart-wrenching. Six-year-old Luke sent me a postcard every time he did anything special, and often when he didn't! One day he wrote: "Dear mum I hope you get better sewn I mis you a lote I wish you kud com dake to englelud it isunt eny fun withot you Love from Luke." Amy's letters were newsy and full of a little girl's fun. How I missed them.

I wrote to each of them individually every week at least once, telling them again and again how much I loved them, and sent a parcel of some kind every other week, with some little token of my love and pride in them. One day I wrote in big letters to both the children using fourteen different coloured pens: "Hi Amy and Luke! How are you doing? Did you know that I think you are both gorgeous, wonderful, marvellous, delicious and I would like to gobble you both up for my dinner. I love you lots and lots and lots and lots. With hugs and (sloppy) kisses from Mummy xxxxxx."

Many such letters crossed the Atlantic. As winter approached I wrote bossy instructions to John, to make sure the children were warm enough at night, to give them plenty of fresh fruit and suggesting he give them vitamin tablets. I reminded him often to cut their fingernails, make sure they brushed their teeth and kept their hair cut and clean. I grappled with not being in control of things that came second nature to me as a mother – the care of her children.

But instead, I had to take care of myself. Sleeping was spasmodic because I was always so hungry. There was little in the kitty left for food. "I am sad today. I have just $10 left, with about $250 in the bank, which may or may not cover the cost of mover's fees... The car needs insurance, plus spare parts – and, of course, gas. I am having my hair cut on Friday, and have run out of postage stamps and deodorant. I need money." I tried to aim at eating one good meal each week so that I could at least function. Amazingly I survived. There was always enough in the end. That was a God thing.

Doug introduced me to a lively church which he felt could be helpful. After attending a few services I felt comfortable enough to relax. Mistake. During the service JuJu came out and trotted over to where Doug was sitting. Just like any little child she wouldn't sit still and eventually left the hall and wandered outside, so I missed the rest of the service. Afterwards she went over to where Doug and the pastor, Pete, were talking and was taken to the back of the stage. They talked to her and calmed her, prayed, then brought me back. Pete didn't seem to have any trouble accepting the presence of another "part" of me. I was to develop a deeply trusting relationship with Pete, and in his gentle way he invited many of the alters to come and speak with him in the days and months ahead. JuJu in particular liked his company and it was seldom that I spent time with him without JuJu muscling in on the conversation. I would be talking away when suddenly (it was always "suddenly" with JuJu) I would be back on the inside looking out and she would be stammering and stuttering her way through some tale or other using her arms to emphasize her point. Pete appeared to have no problem with that. He was a large man, rather like a jolly Father Christmas, and JuJu and other child alters affectionately called him "Big Pete".

She was beginning to hint more frequently about the "troubles" she had. Often she would appear and say to whoever was listening, "I have troubles."

"What are your troubles, JuJu?"

"I'm not all that very good at telling them to people," she would reply. She was always very reluctant to say exactly what they were because she had to be a "good girl". She had done something very bad, and expected people to be constantly "cross" with her. She would sometimes ask "Chrisfer" if he was going to hurt her.

"No, I'm not going to hurt you, JuJu. Have I ever hurt you before? I like you, I would never hurt you. I don't hurt little girls. Some people do hurt them, but I would never hurt you."

"You're a nice man."

"There are lots of nice men. There are some bad men too, but lots of nice men. You are safe now."

It was so important to her that people think she is good. "Am I a good girl yet, Chrisfer?" But she never really heard his response of reassurance, the fear was far too deep to be dispelled just with a kind word. She had been told that if she ever told of these things she must take a knife and cut her own throat.

There were times when JuJu, speaking of the bad things that happened to her, appeared to be reliving the unpleasant event, as if she were still there.

"The sky's a long way away. It's black. It's too big in here. Will someone come and touch me, touch me here?" (She touches her cheek.) "It's black and it's black and it's black.

Anybody, don't go away. Anybody, don't go away. Anybody, don't go away. Anybody, please come. Anybody, please come and then I'll be good, and then I'll be very good. Please don't go away. It looks like everybody's going away and it's just me. Mummy. Mummy. Mummy…"

Christopher gently intervenes, "Would you like me to be there…?"

"It's messy. It's all sticky. I'm mud in a puddle."

"It's all right."

"Will you touch me?" JuJu touches her cheek. Christopher does so.

"Can you tell me what happens now? You're remembering. I'm right here. You can talk about it."

As JuJu continues to work through the memory she becomes distressed. Christopher remains calm and his voice is soft, "You're remembering. You're remembering. Feel my hand. I'm right here."

There were many memories of painful, abusive and utterly disgusting events. JuJu recounted the details: the green squared pattern of the carpet, the rope that was dirty, the sound of their laughing, the spider on the lamp, a man's red neck scarf.

By the summer of 1990 I was part of a stable church and had a strong friend in Heide, the missionary at Link Care who appeared that night I had been so low. Things were definitely looking up. I had even received some food vouchers from a Christian charity. But therapy was getting more unpredictable and the pain of recounting the memories was increasing. Cutting myself with razors was becoming a way of releasing the pain – because as I saw the blood I could "see" the pain that was inside and otherwise unseen.

One day I was struggling to believe that all this was real, and felt I must be a really bad, bad person for behaving the way I did – other parts of me doing and saying childish and shocking things. I cut my arms until the blood flowed freely. But now that the alters had found a safe place in Link Care and a safe person in Christopher it was difficult for me to hide; somebody, an alter, would come out and tell on me.

I was at Heide's house at one of these times; she and Edmundo had gone to work. JuJu came out and promptly marched over to the Link Care office two minutes away, arms dripping blood, where the long-suffering receptionist washed my wounds and we waited for Christopher to finish an appointment. Those receptionists were wonderful, forever patient and kind, facing the most bizarre behaviour with calmness and wisdom. Several times I had to go to the hospital for stitches, usually met with open disapproval – "self-harmers are not acceptable and not welcome in emergency rooms. They don't deserve to receive decent treatment. If they want to cut themselves up they have to take the consequences" is the kind of attitude I encountered. Fair enough.

During the worship time on Sundays I regularly fell over and "checked out". Usually JuJu would come out and explain: we have "troubles", but I always felt embarrassed. One Sunday there was opportunity for any who wanted it to go forward for deliverance prayer. A friend beside me suggested I receive prayer right where I was, but that was all too much for JuJu. She went away to the inside and was replaced by "Meg", a four-year-old alter created to escape, who always took her shoes and socks off before making a quick getaway. In the heat of the moment, with Meg on the floor struggling with her socks, one of the elders whisked me up in his arms like a child and sped off quietly to the side to calm the inside down.

In a few months the image I had of myself as a sane Christian woman, albeit one with a secret, had been turned on its head. Now I was a whole multitude of people, acting in inappropriate ways. In my journal I recorded: "I feel such a fool, I must believe in myself as a responsible, mature woman, not as a blithering idiot."

Who was I really? Would I ever be whole? I was very literally falling apart: could God ever put me together again? I had lost my husband and children because of this, and the people around me were still strangers to me.

There is no way I could return to my family in England any time soon. It wouldn't be safe. What if the satanists who had hurt me found out I had been telling on them? What if there was nobody in England who understood Multiple Personality Disorder? What if the alters made sure I didn't arrive alive? My family were no longer the OK people I thought, as many of them were implicated in the emerging stories and memories. All I had left was God.

Very early one morning I was lying in my sleeping bag on the floor of Pat's spare room. I felt as though everything had been stripped from me. Other people's things surrounded me, not mine. I had nothing. My car had just died, my few second-hand clothes were looking distinctly shabby, I had no food, no money, no home, no family and few friends. I was illegal in a foreign land, and even my sanity was on the cards. All the fight in me had gone, and I was ready for surrender.

But...

I still had a Saviour. Jesus had chosen me to be his own. And I knew that I knew that I knew that I was his. If I were ever to come out of all this mess it would have to be his doing, his salvation, his deliverance. Nothing and no one else would be big enough to rescue me. A growing sense of peace and well-being filled me like the gradual rising of dawn on a black and barren landscape. Fingers of rose-coloured light warmed gently through me until I felt a surge of hope blossoming as in an emerging day. "It's going to be all right. I know it's going to be all right."

Chapter
10

Developments

On the inside Meg had very short, thick fair hair and wide eyes. Although she had a deep need for touch and affection she was generally suspicious and uneasy. Each alter had a job to do, and her function in my inside system was to get me away from the scene of abuse; she would run at the first opportunity. Of course, as an adult I no longer needed to run away; there was nothing to run from and nowhere to run to. But Meg hadn't grasped that, in spite of Christopher's continual reassurances. She hated wearing anything cumbersome like coats and sweaters, shoes and socks, and off they came as soon as she was out, in preparation for the great escape. Therapy proved difficult when Meg first came because she immediately tried to run out of the door. So Christopher devised an ingenious way of curbing her escape tactics. Working on the principle that alters are generally very suggestible, he tied a "sleep string" to the door handle. If Meg or any of the alters were to touch the handle with the string on it, he explained, they would immediately fall asleep.

It worked. From then on Meg was able to be contained enough to stay and tell what she needed to. It was to be years before she really felt safe enough to come out without tugging off her shoes and socks "just in case". But Meg was not a good girl. She ran and made a fuss, and that was dangerous stuff. Her coming made things harder for JuJu, who was so frantic that we might do something bad – the most dreaded punishment for her was not physical pain but rejection and abandonment. She couldn't bear that and lived in terror of being left alone.

JuJu quickly became very attached to Christopher. Holding his hand when recalling horrid things helped to ground her – she struggled during these times to distinguish past from present; it felt as though the bad things were still happening, and only with physical contact, a gentle touch, could she be brought back to the safety of the present.

In the summer of 1991 Christopher went on holiday for three weeks. That was a tough time for JuJu. Actually, many of the alters were afraid he would abandon us and never return. The night before he left the country I recalled in my journal that JuJu cried herself to sleep saying: "I don't have a mummy and I don't have a daddy. All I have is a Chrisfer and now he's gone away."

I felt unmotivated and depressed for much of the time he was away. He represented safety and understanding. Now there was none. It didn't help that I didn't have enough money for food, and was sometimes very hungry, adding to a growing sense of deprivation. Cutting my arms and legs became an option which I chose too often, and when he found out, "Big Pete" was angry. One day he told JuJu that if she cut he would not allow her to come to church. That sounded harsh and uncaring. He clearly didn't understand, I thought, and I did what I had to anyway. JuJu felt overwhelmed and accused: "I will try to be good, I will try to be good." But sometimes other alters did things JuJu would not dare to.

On Christopher's return from his holiday we presented him with a large picture that many of the alters had contributed to (you can see a picture of it in the centre pages). JuJu was very excited at the prospect of seeing him again, but at the same time struggled with the possibility that he may at any time go away again and not come back. Feelings were raw, and unsteady. My self-ness seemed under attack as I became increasingly aware of the inner fragmentation. The whole of life was scary and unsafe and oozing painfully. I was writing strange things in my journal:

> The me inside me has gone. On Wednesday night I was at Rob's potluck and lots of other people were there. They were not me, they were apart from me. But I couldn't find a "me" to relate to them... the inside me had gone away and was no longer here. I was empty and void. But I am not any of the "others"; they are them and not me. Now I don't know what to do... after a sleep I prayed and each time had to go and vomit (such was the repulsion I felt for all of this stuff). I don't know what to do.

In August 1990 I went to live at Link Care with Heide and her family. By now something I called the "No" episodes had settled into our routine: my head was chock-full and overflowing with the word "No". It flowed out of my hands whenever a pen or pencil was in them, and out of my mouth when there was appropriate opportunity. "Something bad, dangerous, evil has got to stop. I don't want this. No. No. No." I filled dozens of sheets of paper with that word. "No. No. *No.* Not me. *Not me.*"

I was believing a lie. The lie was that it was still happening. "No, *No.*" The lie was that I would always have to do what I didn't want to do. "No, *No.*" The lie was that life is bad and I would have to fight against everything, forever. "No, *No.* No more. *No more.* Please no more. *Please stop.* I will be good. No. No. Go away. *I will be good.* No. No..."

I didn't know that I was now utterly and completely safe in the arms of Almighty God, my true and eternal Father. I hadn't realized that complete freedom is now mine. I hadn't yet been introduced to the delightful "Yes" of God's love and acceptance.

Twice a week for an hour and a half each session, Christopher would sit with me as I and my alters recounted stories. Many, many times it would get to the end of the session and I would "come back" feeling exhausted but without knowing exactly what had been said, though I often had a vague and general idea. There were feelings of panic and revulsion lingering in the pit of my stomach, and sometimes unbelievably brutal, far-away pictures would tantalize me for a few moments at a time and then vanish. So we began to routinely audiotape the sessions and I would go home, wherever that happened to be, and listen with a thumping heart to the session's events.

Towards the end of a memory work session JuJu would usually come out in distressed panic.

"I don't know what to do, I don't know what to do, Chrisfer, I don'knowhatodo, I don'knowhatodo, I don'knowhatodo."

"And what do you do when you don't know what to do?"

"I have to be good, I have to be good."

"You are a good girl, JuJu, you are a good girl. You don't have to do anything, you know that? You're safe now."

"Am I a good girl yet?"

"Yes. Yes. You've always been a good girl, JuJu."

"It doesn't feel very nice."

"It's all right not to feel very nice. That was bad what they did to you. It's all right not to feel good. But you're safe now. That happened a long time ago. It's not happening now. You're safe now."

JuJu would whine softly, her pain dissipating until she was able to go back inside, now comforted.

I had a job of sorts. Pete asked me to be a research assistant for him. His hour-long sermons were packed full of inspiration and facts and he preached twice each Sunday. I spent many rich hours poring over commentaries and study books digging out juicy morsels for his sermons. Oh the joy of that!

I could escape from the intensity of therapy, the pain of bad "stuff" and enter another world. Jesus was there. He walked out of the pages, and into my head. I studied the Beatitudes and fairly revelled in Jesus' gracious words and the beauty and eternity I found in them. Pete gave me some wonderful books to use – *Vine's Expository Dictionary, Wilson's Old Testament Word Studies, Young's Concordance*. I felt important; I had a positive job to do, one with kingdom consequences. Those hours poring over the word of God provided an oasis in the searing heat of the desert. The word of God is a soothing ointment, a balm, a delicious taste, a precious possession. I hope I never underestimate its power to calm and heal.

One day during the worship at an evening service a new alter came out. The worship leader had said he felt there were some who felt they were "nothing". At that, deep, tearless sobs began to erupt from inside me; I couldn't contain them. As they increased in volume my whole body shook and I knew I had to leave or else be disruptive. By the time we were far away down the empty corridor I allowed myself to let go. I stood against the wall and, sure of my solitude, violently let out the stifled wails. Doug, who appeared from nowhere, approached calmly and gently. "You are very sad. What's your name?" The loud wails and cries stopped suddenly. "Nothing," she whispered.

"Nothing" came to speak with Christopher in therapy a few days later and we learned of her story. She revealed that I was eight-years-old when she came and was created to keep me out of the way and out of sight. I felt of no account, of no importance, a non-person. I could be made use of by others because it didn't matter what happened to me. I was a nobody, nothing. Another lie was revealed and embodied; another battle to fight in my mind. I didn't matter, not to anybody. I would never matter.

During that same service Pete asked for volunteers to be

part of a support team for a church member. He described the situation in some detail without mentioning any names. He would carefully vet them and would be choosy in his selection. They were to be of help emotionally and spiritually for this vulnerable church member. I was so surprised when it eventually dawned that he was speaking about me. From then on I had a group of incredibly supportive and loyal friends who helped in a million ways, from taking me shopping to praying with me, from buying me coffee and doughnuts to giving me a car.

The members of my support network occasionally joined me in therapy with Christopher. Not all my support team was from Pete's church. I had known Vivian, and David her husband, since "Agape" days and valued her friendship enormously. As she lived further north, in the next town, I didn't see her very often but my times with her were filled with stimulating conversation about creativity and beauty. God gave me some wonderful people who loved and refreshed me. Viv instilled in me the growing desire to put down on paper what was in my head, not just the bad stuff but all the excitement and wonder of being alive in a beautiful, God-filled world. I wanted to catch her love of life, her vibrancy and zest. She was a gift from heaven to me. I loved to be with her. Viv was so open to the alters and loved them as she loved me. She wrote once to me:

"I found it fascinating, especially Ju-Ju. Each of the main alters were so complete, so convincing as to their ages and personalities. Amazing. Yes, I was curious but it seemed perfectly natural. I don't think I ever doubted that they were real. The room you imagined or saw inside you with the alters there waiting to go out to speak, was especially fascinating." God was giving me some very special people, and I was learning to appreciate and bless them.

By now the number of alters I put in the maps of my inner

world was mounting dramatically. They came to uncover the secrets of my past and my distorted thinking. By March 1991 sixty-one alters had revealed themselves. I had been drawing these "maps" of the inside for some time for Christopher to see who I was made up of, and regularly needed to update them as I discovered more about the system and how it worked. We were well organized – this was no random collection of parts shuffling for space in my head. In common with most people with MPD I was very well ordered and had rules and etiquette to be broken at my peril!

Each alter related to the others who were near him or her on the inside, and many were arranged in clusters according to their function. So the angry bunch were together, the very young ones, those who were particularly loyal to the cultic group that used us, etc. A few were isolated and knew very little of the other alters. Most of them were aware of me as the host personality and one to be protected at all costs, mainly from knowing the truth about the abuse. The whole point of the separate parts, separated by walls of amnesia, was to keep me from ever knowing what ghastly things men and women had chosen to inflict on me. They each had a role and a purpose, however minor, and almost all of them aggressively stuck to that role.

"Pieces" came when the abusers had put a blanket round my face and spun me round and round and round. Sometimes she was tied up in a hessian sack and spun. She was constantly confused, constantly frightened. Unaware of the present, she carried me all the times when we were blindfolded and disoriented before ritual abuse took place.

Then there was "Daggers". He turned out not to be an alter after all, but was just posing as one. Christopher was not deceived for long. If you expose the whole of yourself to the Light, it does not take long to figure out where the darkness is. He was cast out by Pete and his team as the demon he was.

He/it did not respond to love and kindness. Alters are love-starved parts of a hurting person. They are looking for affirmation and understanding, and will, in time and with patience, warm to affection when it is gently and consistently offered. Demons don't. Demons come from the enemy and will reveal their true nature when exposed to the light of God's love.

"Stephanie" had been created to identify with the object of worship and evil power, and at first was deeply committed to satanism and all it stood for. She was originally named "Satan" after her master. She was told in the satanic group that she had special powers and was promised privileges, but was tricked. At first, on "coming out" she was very angry with satanists, and with everyone else; she was full of hate. But she came to meet Jesus in "Big Pete"'s office and the change in her was profound. From that moment on she couldn't understand why Christians were not all radically Christ-focused and walking in the power of the Holy Spirit. She was impressed with the story of Stephen's courage and faith in Acts and wanted to change her name to Stephen after him. It was explained to her that she might like a girl's name, as she was perceived to be a girl like Carolyn. So she became Stephanie.

Throughout our times with Christopher we were encouraged to work together at communicating on the inside. He pointed out that it would be good for us all to listen-in when an alter was telling his/her story – that it's now safe, and no harm will come to us from telling or from knowing. There was once a time when it was very important that we didn't know what had happened; that knowing meant danger or being so overwhelmed with pain and grief that we wouldn't survive. But now it was different. We're safe and strong, and our goals now are to uncover the grisly truth of what's happened to us, so that it's no longer a powerful secret. We can look at it and face the past for what it is – old memories of old events. Today is now, and we can choose to live a different way and believe different things. We were once powerless and vulnerable, but now we were in a position to make choices. We had control over our life.

Once the stories were told we could think about becoming one whole person, rather than a collection of separate parts. That is called "integration", but at this stage we were a long way from such a bold step.

The support group were beginning to ask me out for meals and trying to help in practical ways. I was living with a nurse who worked nights, Leanne from the church. I was so grateful for her offer of accommodation in her little clapboard house of only three tiny rooms, but was under strict instructions to make absolutely no sound during the day. I wasn't able to use the kitchen of course – so no meals. Not difficult anyway, because I had no money for food. I also felt that I was under pressure to be a really good girl for everyone – to be super-duper grateful even though at that stage there were some members of my support team I didn't yet know or had never met. It's hard to show gratitude for something you haven't yet received. So things felt awkward.

Memories began to surface regarding our being taken to another location, not connected at all to the old church where the early memories of abuse in the bell tower took place, but a large house. We remembered the car wheels crunching on the gravel drive, and being led into a dimly lit hallway. All the spacious rooms were almost empty – maybe it was a derelict house, I don't know. There were other grown-ups in the house, some of them had clothes on and some didn't. The place was very quiet, nobody spoke very loudly; it all seemed clinical and cold. I was expected to know what to do and when to do it. JuJu was always there and always nervous.

Another set of memories occurred around a field of long grass near our home. It was really a large patch of open waste ground, with a fence on one side and a house belonging to a cousin on another. A whole gang of young child alters were created to deal with these memories, with names like "Twinkle", "Jenny Wren", "Hands", "Sunshine", "April". It was after one of the times of recalling these situations that "Cherub" introduced herself. She was a confident, well-spoken seven-year-old alter who wanted to make it quite plain from the outset that she was an "observer", and spoke the word with great emphasis! She was proud to tell Christopher that she "observed things" and so never really felt she was being abused herself. She was a valuable ally to have in therapy as she could tell of unspeakable things without emotion, therefore didn't have to "check out" and bring another alter in when it got too much. Stormie was sometimes angry with Cherub because in her eyes she said too much. But even Cherub would not disclose the identities of the abusers, in common with many of the alters. There was no way any of them would disclose that information for a long, long time.

It was spring 1991 and the alters were increasingly trusting Christopher; there was a sense of general safety on the outside too. Even though Leanne had asked us to leave and find somewhere else to live (she was moving to another state), there was a feeling that God had taken care of us so far and so would continue to. There was still a big issue around food – I did not get enough of it and was getting very thin and weak. I weighed only six stone. Nevertheless I was ready to face the next trauma.

We knew that two-year-old "Little Joey" was an inner representative of a baby who had been seen in one of the rituals. JuJu told that he had been under a dark green blanket on the table. She was convinced she had been very, very bad, and it had something to do with Little Joey.

"There was no light 'cept on the table. It's candles. Grown-ups are there and I come from the 'nother room. I have some cloes on. Not my cloes. I don't have undies on 'cos there's a man who likes me – he has big fingers. There's a lump on the table. It moved 'cos it was a baby underneath. It was little Jonathan, he is just a little baby. There's a chair and I have to stand on it. They have a knife. They didn't touch it to me. They say things in a funny voice. I have to take the knife and put it there (she touches her throat) of the baby. I didn't do it right. Then the blood spilled out the bowl. They catched it in a bowl, the blood. They were cross wiz me." Her voice rises to a high pitch of panic. "Chrisfer, they were cross wiz me. They were cross wiz me. Chrisfer, Chrisfer. I will be good. I will be good…"

She became agitated and upset, her stiff, tense body squirmed and jerked as she sat on the edge of her seat gripping Christopher's hand. Her eyes were tightly shut, her forehead deeply frowning and her head tilted upwards as if she were trying to hear or see something from far away. He gently and softly reassured her, "You are safe. I am here. You're just remembering. It's all right".

"They get cross wiz me."

"But that's not your fault. They're cross people. Angry people get angry, don't they? If they're cross inside they'll get angry on the outside too, won't they? It had nothing to do with you. You were a good girl doing the best you could. Will you remember that?"

It was soon after that I, overwhelmed with the implications of that memory, overdosed – well, somebody did but as it was my mouth and my stomach that were involved I had to take the consequences. Somehow or other (did an alter ring him?) Bruce (from my support group) got to know, drove over and took us to the hospital. I had to drink a thick and foul cup of what tasted, and looked, like black tar. After hours sitting on a gurney (the American term for a hospital trolley or stretcher on wheels) in an overcrowded, chaotic and noisy hospital corridor I was eventually released.

Suddenly everything seemed so precarious. As I had to leave Jannette's I was offered a room with another couple in the church. But they didn't have me for long. There was a church split and they, along with a sizeable number of others, left the fellowship. It somehow didn't feel right for me, so committed to Pete and his close group, to stay with people who chose to leave the church. So once again I had to seek somewhere to live.

I was always hungry. Very hungry. Whenever money came my way I would want to spend it on Amy and Luke. That was my one pleasure – to wander round the shops to see what funky toy or amusing game I could afford to send them. More usually it was stickers and pencils, but I tried to find creative ways of sending them, wrapped in interesting paper, or in a box packed out with "cheetos", a light, cheesy snack that looks rather like edible polystyrene. They were still my pride and joy, and not even my hunger could prevent me from doing what mothers love to do, lavish their affections on their children. They were a long way away, but I could still find ways of showing them I loved them with all my heart.

How to keep alive was a major concern. I prayed in, it seemed, every morsel, and became weary of being so grateful even for a cup of coffee. The people around me were eating and drinking all they wanted to, all the time, every day. That was tough. Should I ask them for food? That was so very hard and didn't seem right at all. I wish I had realized that we can ask God for big things – I wouldn't have been "bad" for asking and expecting him to provide food *all* the time. So I continued to live in hope rather than expectation. I would later learn that he is a super-generous God; we can dare to ask for all our needs to be fulfilled. But for that sort of faith I would have to wait.

Chapter
11

Depravity

CS Lewis, in his sermon "The Weight of Glory", wrote something quite telling, that finds resonance in me: "We are half-hearted creatures, fooling about with drink and sex and ambition when infinite joy is offered us, like an ignorant child who wants to go on making mud pies in a slum because he cannot imagine what is meant by the offer of a holiday at the sea. We are far too easily pleased."

I was always sure that God wanted to give me more than the life I was presently experiencing. Not that "drink, sex and ambition" were high on my agenda, but I was sure it was OK to be dissatisfied. I was able to keep on going with this weary tramp through hostile territory because I was sure there was, somewhere, a life that touched on the divine, that was washed with a calm that was, as yet, outside of my experience. I just knew that God has a quality of life in store for us that was waiting to be enjoyed. I simply had to keep on going until I found it.

JuJu, often the first one to speak of a bad memory, was learning that our safety is ultimately in God. She had come to trust in Jesus as her friend. Our videotaped sessions revealed these conversations:

"Chrisfer, Carolyn said I had to tell you zings... but they're not nice zings."

"I understand."

"But you won't go away?"

"I will be here the whole time. Have I ever gone away when we've talked together like this? Molly (her furry rabbit) will be here and… "

"And Jesus will be here."

"That's right. And Jesus will be here."

One day, at the end of a session we were videotaping, Christopher asked me if I knew the names of any of the abusers. Something in my mind snapped and I lost the words in my head. A bomb went off and scattered the words untidily around my brain. I tried but I couldn't gather them up. An alter came out, and started to pace wildly up and down. She flung Molly onto the floor, kicked a chair and threw a cup of water in the air in anger.

"This is stupid, i'n'it? It's all stupid. It's stupid, Christopher."

"Who am I talking to now?"

"Du'nt ma'er does it?"

"Sure it does."

"It's stupid. Stupid." She crashes the blinds wildly.

"Do you understand, you need to be able to express your anger, and I accept that, but if you damage anything that's not going to be tolerated."

"It's stupid." She kicks the chair and throws a doll across the room.

"You want to talk to me? What's your name?"

"Dun't ma'er does it?"

"It matters a lot. It matters to me. You're important to me. But we have to talk. We can't simply throw things around. I understand you feel that way, OK? I accept that. But it's not appropriate to throw things around. That's not going to help us to feel better."

The unknown and irate alter with rather a lot of energy and passion continues to pace around and crashes the blinds again. Christopher continues, "I asked the wrong question today, huh? D'you need to talk? You can talk about your anger as much as you want, OK? But you've got to express it appropriately. You can't break things. That's not going to help Carolyn, that's not going to help her to get better, OK?"

She sits defiantly on the sofa.

"Now, I'd love to talk to you. You're important to me. You're important to Carolyn. You helped her survive. And you're welcome to talk with me, and help me understand why you were created. Do you have a name?"

"Yeh."

"My name's Christopher. The first part of getting to know someone is getting to know their name."

"Can't tell you."

"Why can't you tell me? You don't want to? If you don't want to, that's one thing… "

"Not s'pposed to."

She wouldn't give her name but said she was created when I was six-years-old. Christopher spoke of how JC used to be angry but now feels good.

"She's gone religious."

"But is she happier? Does she seem to enjoy life now? Think about those things."

"She's just suckin' up to everyone."

"I don't think so… she was very angry once, too. But she and I worked together. We talked, and she's glad where she is now. Would you like to have a relationship to me and others like JC has? Think of that."

"Nob'dy 'd want me."

"I'm talking to you now, aren't I? If you were so terrible I wouldn't be talking to you."

"Well, you 'ave to."

"Oh, I have to. Sure. No, I don't have to. I could have

someone else come out. I could say, 'I don't want to talk to this one', but I did. I..."

"It's stupid."

"I'd like to do that some more if it's possible."

"It's stupid."

"Think about what I've said."

We later learnt that her name was "Becky", and she was part of a whole group of angry alters, headed up by JC who then came and explained who Becky was and why she was there. The angry alters, most of whom were teenagers we had already met, were named: "Terror", "Stormie", "JC", "Becky", "Panda", "The Searcher" (later named Mary), and "Honesty".

Becky's anger was to continue even after she made a commitment to Christ. She spoke of what it was like growing up:

"People didn't know, see. You 'ave to 'old it in, see, 'cos it's secret. It's not fair, see, that people don't know. It's not fair, Christopher. F...parents, I 'ate 'em. I'm not going back to England. Never, not ever. I'm not going to 'ave nuffin to do with 'em. I'm not goin' to write to 'em or nuffin'. F...parents. I 'ate 'em. We weren't like uvver kids, see. They fought we were, but we weren't."

"I know that," Christopher reassures her. "Somebody knows that now. That's the first step."

"We couldn't tell no one."

"That's right, you couldn't tell anyone. But now things have changed. The body's older. You are very important. You helped take some of the pain that Carolyn couldn't handle. That's the whole point, you all need each other."

"See, I've gotta be good now, I'm not allowed to curse and stuff cos I'm Christian an' that."

"What happens here, I accept, OK?"

With her London accent, she had a fair amount of rough and ready wisdom and loved to tell jokes; some, it has to be

Three years old with my sister, in one of the aunties' gardens.

Age five, on a family outing.

Smiling for the camera:
a school photograph
when I was six.

Seven years old and posing in
my ballet outfit.

I am the one on the right – and I was so much smaller than my sister I had to sit on a high stool for the school cameraman.

Our first home together. John and I used it as a meeting place for the young people we led and prayed for.

A happy little family, just before we left for America. Amy was six and Luke was three years old.

Our second Christmas in California would have been very frugal had some kind friends not stepped in.

A moment of silly fun at our ranch home.

A pensive moment. Amy and Luke knew they would soon be leaving their mummy behind in America while they returned to England with John.

All packed up and ready to go: the children and I wait outside the hotel for the taxi to take us all to San Francisco airport. It would be three and a half years before I would see them again.

JuJu in America in 1991. She would be the last alter to integrate. Note the cheerful clothing, her tense posture, and the fact that she didn't need glasses – in fact she had 20/20 vision, unlike myself.

23 alters were baptised on one amazing day. JC, here, was the first to take the plunge.

Becky, please   Carolyn.

I don't think Christopher ever has rows with
anybody. He probably just reads the newspaper
till its all over.   Stormie

No, probly a boring psychology book!
                                                Becky

With no pictures in and no comics or anything!
                                                Stormie.

I think we need to get back on track here. Ju Ju, do you feel
better now about Dr. Brent?   Carolyn.

WIL HE BE KROS IF I DO
IT RONG.

You don't do anything wrong Ju Ju, and Dr Brent,
just like Christopher, is here to make us feel
good. To make it safe. You'll be alright. We'll
all see to that.
                                                Erica.

Im not fritenedJu Ju. You can stay y with me. I will look dafter you. Janey.

SHAll WE ET M anb M Ju Jy

and Junor mints. and lets play. Janey.

do you think I can play too. Cherub

If there's grub I'm going to Join in! That's great you guys We can all look after each other and be one big happy family. Blimey I sound like one of the Brady bunch.
But its ok isnt it? The little kids dont have to be around when Chris is away. Cant you persuade

Two pages from one of my American journals, from 1991/2. Note the way the alters dialogue amongst themselves. Beth, one of the alters, was left-handed: I am right-handed.

Letters and artwork from the alters.

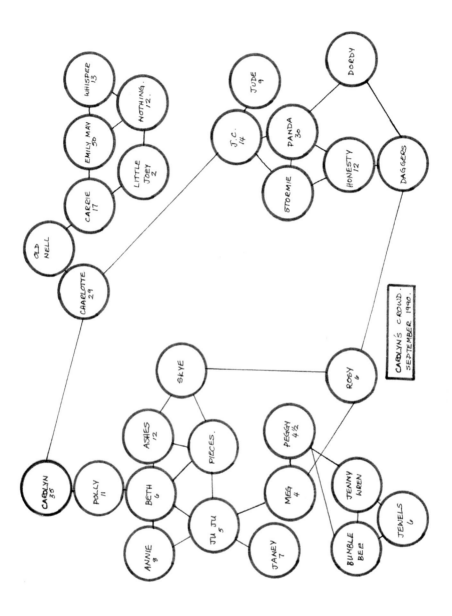

Two years into therapy and we had identified 29 alters. I regularly had to update these maps.

Some good friends came to see me off at San Francisco airport. We didn't know if we would ever see each other again.

United at last! This was taken at Heathrow airport moments after I came through the barrier. How wonderful it was to hold my children in my arms after so long.

I had to sift through piles of letters, photo albums, video and audio tapes, therapy notes and journals in order to piece my story together.

The flat gravestone is still there where Ashes was created after the burning sacrifice incident.

Valentine's Day 1970 was the first day of my new life: the day I met Jesus in this very field. Until recently I could remember nothing before that date.

A friendly send off. I left the Friendship Clubs to spend time on my work with Freedom in Christ. I have since started a new branch of the Clubs.

Pals together. Amy and I picnicking recently on a summer's day.

The Walking with the Wounded team, part of the Freedom in Christ team. A great bunch of people.

Christopher Rosik, my American therapist and now a good friend, whose support saw me through some very dark times. His notes on the case and my condition appear in the Appendix.

Steve and Zoë Goss of Freedom in Christ Ministries have proved invaluable. Their love, encouragement and prayers made a vital difference. Steve's Afterword gives his perspective.

Amy and Luke have now left home, but we are still very much together as a family in the ways that count.

said, in rather dubious taste. Becky was rather less than compassionate at first when it came to understanding other, more distressed alters. She thought "Polly", who took our depression, "just a misery-guts". She found Ashes particularly difficult to accept. "She's weird. She's spooky. She dun't know about you an' stuff. Can't I just be me? Can't I just be thirteen? I don't want anything to do with all of this stuff, with Ashes and that."

"You can't get away from the body, you can't get away from the whole. We all need to work together."

"But there's loads of this stuff. I don't like it a' all."

"But we'll get through it."

The feelings from the alters were leaking increasingly through the amnesic barriers to the core me. I wrote in my journal in July: "If I could stop at any time in the day and do whatever I wanted to, I would wail from the pit of my stomach, long and loud, like Ashes."

"Ashes" was twelve-years-old and she, too, struggled to distinguish between the past and the present. She initially came to handle the pain of a particular event involving a ritual in a churchyard. On a tombstone I was strapped, naked, to another child – a school friend – and prepared for what I believed to be sacrifice. It may not, of course, been anything more than intimidation. A short while later I was released and put into a dug grave. Then something or somebody I couldn't see was set alight on that same tombstone. Was it my friend? Should that have been me? The rank smelling ashes floated over me in the eerie smoke, and then the limp, hot, black remains were thrown over me.

At some point in all of this Ashes was created to deal with this new trauma. Thereafter she held the memories of confinement – in a coffin, in a grave, in a cellar, in other small, cold, damp spaces. She consequently over-reacted to similar situations, sometimes by being loudly hysterical. Her safe place on the inside is a dry tree hollow from which she can look out over the wide, green countryside.

Ashes was often totally disoriented when she came into our body and sometimes would wander around the room in some distress. She really thought she still had the chain around her neck. She needed lots of gentle reassurance from Christopher that she was now safe:

"It's OK. It's Christopher. Do you know where you are? There's nowhere to go. Do you remember me? I won't hurt you. There's nowhere to go. It's OK."

Ashes released ear-piercing screams and wails as a way of expressing her pain, sounds she had been too afraid to release when she was being tied and confined and hurt. Those heart wrenching, soul-stabbing shrieks had been locked away deep within her psyche and now she was at last allowed to give vent to them. She recounted being locked in a coffin, naked. We taped some of the sessions with Ashes, she sounded like a wounded animal. "Aaaahhgg!" As I listened to the tape after- wards a shock of ice-cold terror shot through me like frozen lightning. My mouth went dry. She continued to scream, shrill, piercing. Then a frantic "Get me out. Get me out. Get me out... Get me out of here. Get them off me."

"It's the blood that gets to you," she was later to explain. "They cut you so that it doesn't show, so that no one will see... they tie up my heart. They squeeze it. They tie it up inside me. They do it so I won't breathe when I tell." She was fighting for her safety, for her sanity, for her life. I didn't always understand what she was talking about, I didn't have to understand it all. I knew that it had been bad; very bad.

Ashes wasn't the only one worried about blood. "Elizabeth" was terrified too. She saw something that so blighted her mind that the least suggestion of blood sent her frantic with terror. In order for Christopher to help her reframe these events she needed to tell her story too.

As all this was happening on the inside I struggled to cope with the guilt of not being the wife I was created to be, and the mother I longed to be. The children sent me letters and postcards detailing, at first, every event in their lives. I wanted to know it all, and it was never quite enough that they told me what they had eaten for dinner or which friends were off school with the latest tummy bug. But each letter was priceless. Luke was not always one for long tomes, unlike his sister. One day he wrote: "Dear Mummy, It was a good day at school. Love Luke." And another: "Dear Mummy, I love you a lot. I had my picture taken just like I said. I love you very, very, very, very, very, very much. Love from Luke." (Actually it said: "Dear mummy I love you a lote I hade mi piktur tukun gust like I sede…") There were times when he obviously needed his mum. One letter, again pretty to the point, travelled across the ocean to tell me: "Dear Mummy, I am not feeling very well. Love from Luke"! He wanted me to know about Amy's ailments too: "Dear Mummy, Thank you for your letter. Just a few days ago Amy was sick and thank you for my hat. Love Luke."

Amy often had more to say. One day she wrote to invite me to her slumber party, adding "I shure do miss you". Amy felt the need to give me the run-down on all the events in her life, a fact that of course enthralled and delighted me. I was thanked for every item I sent her and told how she used it and when, often as afterthoughts adding three or four "PS"s. She always added notes like: "Please come home very, very, very soon cause I miss you lots." Occasionally she needed to remind me she was growing up: "Dear Mummy, Thank you for the Burger-king comic. I like it, so does Luke. How are you doing? I am doing just fine. I can't remember wich doll I gave you. Also next time you write to me please write in cursive. Now Daddy lets me go to the Post-box on Uplands Way by myself. If Luke wants to come he has to hold my hand.

Lots of Love from Amy!!!!!!!!!"

"Dear Mum, Thank you for putting "mum" instead of "mummy". Also I don't play with dolls any more. How are you? I'm fine. I've just recently changed my best colours. (They were hot pink and purple.) Now it's: black, light blue and white. Red is nice too." This time she went on to describe her sporting achievements and then added at the end: "Please, please, please, please, please, please come home soon!" Their simple pleas for my return cut me deeply.

In one letter Luke added to his short epistle of "Dear Mummy, I hope you are having a good time in America" no less than fifteen "I love you"s. I got the point. Not all his letters were so brief.

"Dear Mummy I miss you very very very very very much. Stuart (his cousin) is still a bit little. I have a cricket bat and I don't use it very much because nobody plays with me that much. i hope you had a nice easter. Thank you for the easter present. i have a lot of chocolate. Amy has more than me but i am waiting until Amy catches up with me because i only have little bits left. One Sunday i saw Grandad in a parade. i want to be in a band a lot. Love Luke x x x x x x x x x x x x x x x x x x x x x x x x x x x x x x x x x x x "

When he was still only six he sent me a full A4-side of writing, with the barest-of-bare spaces between the words. It was all about Valentine's cards and granny and grandad and his prowess with the football and his activity book of ninety-five pages, of which he had already done forty.

I was such a long, long way from my children. Sometimes the pain would grip me and the tears flow long and hard. I had failed them. When they climbed into bed at night there would be no mummy to tuck them in. Every fibre of my being ached to be with them, but that would be impossible. I could not, ever, go back to England. I would die.

But life was, of course, moving on for them, and I was fast becoming a distant memory. Every little detail of their lives that I was able to glean from them and from John I savoured. I enjoyed sending them newsy letters and always tried to make them interesting and stimulating. I would include facts and bits of information about where I was living: "Dear Amy… I am living right now with an older couple who have seven children, though they are all grown up now, who were missionaries in Thailand. Do you know where Thailand is? It's way over in Asia, near Indonesia. Maybe you could look it up on the map. They lived in Bangkok. It is very beautiful there, but the people are very, very poor." I often wrote my letters in coloured felt pens and illustrated them as best I could. I sent them all a stocking full of goodies at Christmas, John too, just as we always did. Each time the children had a good report at school I sent them some small reward. If Luke scored a goal at football or Amy drew a nice picture they also received some sort of "well done" in the post. I looked out for anything to let them know how precious they were. It wasn't difficult. But nothing, nothing could be a substitute for my actual presence, and that I couldn't give them. Not yet. Perhaps not ever – who knows?

Then there were the stays in hospital. Well, that was really the safest place to be when you feel out of control, especially when your family are across the other side of the world – they may as well have been on Mars. Nobody really understood what was going on anyway. Even the hospital staff. But at least they got paid for looking after weird people, and so I didn't feel so bad about using up their time if and when alters came and did whatever it is they had to do. But it has to be said that psyche departments, at least in that city in that part of California, left much to be desired in the "nurturing" department.

I had been feeling very, very unstable and wondering what to do. It seemed as though I often didn't really have any control over what was happening to me or what I did. I knew with my mind that these "other" people were really just a part of me, but they certainly seemed to have some extreme needs that I didn't share. My mind felt overwhelmed with darkness and despair. Trying to make a rational decision about my own welfare in these circumstances, not to mention the whole "no-home, no-money" thing, was hard. So one day I concluded that in order to save my life at the very basic level I needed to be in a safe place. I knew of no other than the hospital. There was no one even in the church able or willing to take on someone as unstable as I was at that time.

The acute ward I had been in before had been a paying one not a state one, and even that was no picnic. But I was desperate. This time it would have to be the state hospital, there was no money for food never mind medical insurance. I was soon to learn that it would be rather more basic than I imagined.

Arriving at triage I explained my situation and was marched, without comment, down a narrow corridor to a tiny, box-like department. There were a couple of hefty police officers and a male nurse lounging in a small office, filling the space, with knees overflowing into the corridor. After a curt exchange I was handed over to them then inched into another very small room further along the corridor. This room had padded walls and contained one chair; the door was lodged open. I was told to stay there. No one asked me anything. Being a good girl I demanded nothing of them, and stayed put.

Some time later, maybe an hour, a loud noise was heard coming from along the corridor; a man shouting. A gurney appeared outside my door bearing a very, very drunk man, swearing and cursing, sweating profusely and smelling strongly of alcohol and stale urine. The gurney filled the width of the corridor, so no one could stand alongside him. I assumed there was a nurse somewhere, but could see none. He was tied down with leather restraints, but still managed to work them lose enough to spit hard in my direction. Now the room was so small there was nowhere to go. I tried to hop out of the range of his spits, but did not have much success, he was remarkably good at aiming. He was one angry man. I later remembered: Jesus was spat upon too.

He was there a long time. One time the nurse untied him and led him to the toilet across the corridor. They left the door open and I had full view of the event. The man continued to curse. After about three hours a doctor came and asked me some basic questions. He didn't smile or reassure me in the least. I was seriously beginning to doubt the wisdom of my decision and tried to tell him that I felt better now and could I please go home. The answer was an unequivocal "No".

It was a full four hours before I was led to the ward, still without comment, in between two enormous Arnold Schwarzenegger-type police officers armed with guns and truncheons. Perhaps they thought I might rise to my full four feet something and do them some harm. Once again a curt exchange left me in the hands of sour-faced staff that seemed to have forgotten how to speak. All my possessions were taken from me, including my Bible, with the brief information that I would see them again when I was discharged.

I asked if I might have something to eat and drink (it had been 112 degrees Fahrenheit outside and I had had nothing for many hours). I was given a stale sandwich and a small plastic cup of water. I also asked if I might have a shower. A nurse took me to a very large circular hall in which were twenty or thirty women, all standing or walking about, many of them agitated and obviously mentally unwell. This was to be my home until I was discharged. On one side of the round hall was a glass-fronted nurses' station, where they were able to see everything that was going on without having to mix with us. Around the edge of the hall were six or eight doors, these were the dormitories, only unlocked at bedtime and locked again the next morning. At one side of the hall and next to the nurses' station was a bare, stone, door-less room in which were two or three showers.

I was given a towel and left. I chose the only shower with a curtain and left my clothes and towel on the floor outside. When I was finished my towel and clothes were gone. No sign of them anywhere. Dripping and humiliated I went to the doorway and searched the swarming mass of women for the nurse. She eventually appeared and went off again to track down the clothing thief. Meanwhile I had to stand, naked and wet, on the bare stone floor, surrounded by wild and pacing women, and wait. After a thousand years she returned with the towel and clothing – a disturbed and curious patient had simply wandered off with them.

When it was bedtime I, along with every other woman, like it or not, was given a compulsory sleeping tablet. But not before I was given the standard enema. This must be the most humiliating event in the whole sorry story. With my back to the door, open wide to the large hall full of women, I was subjected to a most uncomfortable and degrading procedure. It was made worse knowing that across the hall in the nurses' station, watching the whole thing, was a nurse I had worked with when I was running "Agape". I had had to bring in a resident for admission, we became friends and we had even stayed in her home. Now she behaved as though she had never met me, and I glimpsed her looking my way just before being commanded to lie on my side. I sank to an all-time low.

Instead of being shown to a dormitory with all the other patients, a gurney was wheeled into the centre of the round hall, under a lamp, and in full view of the nurses' station. As they had decided to put me on "suicide watch" I was to sleep in the spotlight for the first night. They took my clothes to wash with everyone else's, telling me I may or may not get mine back the next day, but I would have something to wear. They marked every item with a pen in large bold letters. When I got out of the hospital days later I threw away every bit of the marked clothing.

Things hardly got better the following day. We were all herded into the hall at 6 a.m. (I did get my clothes back) and had to wait a couple of hours for breakfast. The canteen led off the hall and was open only at meal times and for two hours in the afternoon; it had a table tennis table, a TV and also opened onto a patio. This was our therapy – watching the smokers smoke and the soaps soap, and, if we were really innovative, walking the small, bare outside yard in 100-degree heat in the hottest part of the day.

I was released after three days after a lot of fuss on my part. I had demanded to see a doctor who, eventually, agreed to see me. A relatively brief chat with an intelligent human being was all it took to secure my release. "What are you *doing* here?" was his question. Even he had to jump a few hoops to get me out. Unfortunately, it was not the last time I was there.

Chapter
12

Disorder

Christopher was infinitely patient with my multiple self, and deserves a medal of the highest honour. It was not, for him, simply a matter of listening to the harrowing stories, either. Nor of having to quieten and reassure the younger child alters or play with them on the floor. An element of physical danger was occasionally present.

In early summer a group of alters in what we called "the Middle" appeared on the scene. They were created because of our experiences with the occult, and many of them were violently opposed not only to our talking with Christopher about the abuse, but to our commitments to Christ. They were bent on sabotaging the therapy, and violently angry with Christopher. One day (I have this on video) I had appeared in therapy with a razor and had a sore and bleeding cut on my arm. Christopher, of course, took away the offending instrument, and needed to firmly re-establish the boundaries. He did not invite any of the Middle alters to come at that point, but made it clear that if any did come out and were violent he would shout "Sleep" and immediately they would fall asleep. Let me remind you that alters are only fragments of my whole self and very, very suggestible.

A little while later JuJu was panicking in the way she did, afraid of what the Middle might do. All of a sudden she was gone and someone lunged heavily and violently at

Christopher. He gasped and boldly shouted, "Sleep", louder than I have ever heard this calm and quiet man say anything before. Immediately she collapsed sideways onto a chair, unconscious. Christopher took a moment to gather himself and then spoke to the inert body. He asked Becky, as one who was usually quite unaffected by emotional outbursts, to come out. She was her usual blunt self:

"Can't we get rid of 'em?"

"We don't want to get rid of them, the ones from the 'Middle'. They're there for a reason."

"But can't we just forget about 'em?"

"They are parts of Carolyn and must work as part of the whole."

"They just want to slice us up." Well, that was true, it seemed that they really did want to cause us harm, along with anyone who tried to help us.

Christopher continued to work with the Middle alters, and one by one he made allies of them as they began to understand that he was on their side – that is, he too wanted to help me, Carolyn. Every alter was created to protect the whole personality, and did it in the best way they knew how. The trouble is, for some, those ways were now redundant. At one point in our lives it was important for us to be seen to be committed to Satan, as our abusers were. If we weren't, we would be in more danger. But in 1991 that was no longer the case, and we were free to make our own choices. Alters are not always aware of the present time, it seemed to many of them that we were still in the sixties and life would be in the balance if we were mixed up with Christian things, or even thought about spilling the beans.

JuJu was often still concerned about our safety.

"She doesn't know."

"Carolyn?"

"Mmmm"

"There's a lot of things Carolyn doesn't know, isn't there? She'll have to know them in time, as we tell our stories. That'll be part of getting better."

"I don't want her to talk about Uncle Bob."

"You don't want her to talk about Uncle Bob?"

"No."

"Why not?"

"Nasty things"

"It's OK, JuJu. We've talked about Uncle Bob before, haven't we? And has anything happened when we talked about him?" JuJu shook her head. "That's right. Nothing's going to happen. He won't hurt you now, OK? It's OK to talk about those things now."

"It doesn't feel very good."

"I know it doesn't feel very good, it feels real scary, doesn't it? But this is a safe place to talk about it. And doesn't it feel better to talk about it even if it's scary sometimes?" JuJu nods.

"I feel frightened."

"Yes, but it will feel better in time."

One time JuJu became very anxious that another uncle, Uncle Charlie, was named. Christopher reassures her, "He told you not to mention his name, didn't he? But you know what? He was lying. He didn't want to be known for the bad things he did to you. He threatened to hurt you, didn't he? But he can't hurt you now. That happened a long time ago."

In June Heide took me down to Anaheim to visit the much-acclaimed Dr James Friesen. A pastor and psychologist, he had written a couple of books about MPD and, being periodically convinced that I was making it all up, I felt that a diagnosis by a leading expert would settle things once and for all. Jim was a very approachable and relaxed chap, oozing good humour and kindness. He actually laughed at the idea that I could be making it all up. After speaking at length with a number of the alters, including, of course, JuJu, he reassured me that MPD was the correct diagnosis for me.

Life was difficult also because of my lack of a stable home. I always had a roof over my head, but nevertheless "I really, really, really need to live in a place I can call my own, a place I can call home. I really, really need to be able to cook my own meals, things that I like to eat, things that are good for me. Then I will eat three meals a day, and function better, and sleep better… I will live my own life instead of being tacked onto the back of someone else's every day."

Where I was presently living was a mile's walk to the bus stop and it was 95 degrees Fahrenheit before nine o'clock in the morning. I was travelling on the bus to a food station, queuing in the heat, along with illegal Mexican immigrants and their swarms of small children, for day-old bread and small bags of beans, rice and tortillas. Having got them home I invariably didn't like what I had – the Hispanic diet was not appetizing to me and my stomach had shrunk so much by this time that it was hard to work up any kind of enthusiasm for unfamiliar food.

The Middle was causing a great deal of agitation in me and in the alters. Razor blades were turning up in unexpected places. JuJu and the small children were frightened and many had stopped coming out even in therapy. I felt as though I was about to explode and it took a great deal of energy to behave in a civilised and normal way. I was sick with anxiety most of the time, having to hold everything in. Christopher was working hard to find a room at the hospital to do some work with the alters from the Middle. We needed somewhere private and secure so that both us (me) and Christopher, and any others involved in deliverance prayer, would be safe. But, in spite of lots of phone calls, that was not possible. It was possible, however, for the hospital to admit me for a recovery time afterwards.

Meanwhile we were put on house arrest! Pete decided that until the issues of the "Middle" had been resolved, we were far too dangerous to be left to live alone and be "at large". Middle alters were cutting me frequently and sometimes threatening others. I knew what was happening but felt over-whelmed and powerless to affect it in any positive way. All I could do was pray that God would intervene at some point. I was out of control. I didn't realize that in Christ I could have power over the enemy myself. I just didn't understand the authority I carried in Christ, over every demon that tried to harass me. For there really were demonic forces controlling the Middle alters, but they were assenting to that. One day I would learn that all Christians, even Christian "parts", can have power over the enemy in the name of Jesus.

I was to stay at the home of a couple from my support team. Van and Susie were away and allowed me to stay there alone. In fact only a chosen few were even allowed to see me. I was not allowed out at all. But why such a harsh sentence? A catalogue of dodgy events had led Pete to deliver this rough justice: an unknown alter had, alarmingly, carved an upside-down cross on my stomach causing enough blood to satisfy them; while waiting at Link Care someone from the inside had, in anger or frustration, thrown a glass of water, kicked plant stands and upturned chairs and tables; while visiting another couple from the team, Dave and Kathleen, we were seen fingering and holding sharp carving knives. When Dave demanded we handed them over he was threatened and a struggle took place in which we both sustained cuts on our hands. Things were clearly unstable. I, as Carolyn, was sub-missive and obedient and feared for my credibility. Only a few days earlier I had given an impressive testimony at a women's meeting. I now felt guilty for losing control of the inside; I felt misunderstood, and once again the victim. Christopher had to search my bags for razor blades each time I went to therapy. Things were getting risky. In my journal I wrote: "My mind is heavy and weighted. It feels as if I'm not really in the present. My feet hurt. I wish I could get rid of a deep, rumbling, strong, angry kind of impulse that doesn't match my mood at all... I want to fall over when I stand up or walk and *just go away*. Somewhere else. Somewhere that is peace, and home, and me."

At the end of August we were able to have the long-talked-about prayer weekend in which the troublesome alters from the Middle would be dealt with. The idea was that we would go to the church centre, a safe and private place, and pray for the Middle alters while I was restrained and so unable to escape or do any damage. I gave my full consent to this, but it still was not a comfortable experience. I felt all along that there might have been a better way. But I am a good girl. I do what I think people want me to do. Anyway I wanted to be free and so was prepared to do whatever it would take.

Pete hired a gurney. This one was equipped for use with violent patients and had leather straps attached to firmly tie them down. Yes, just like the one the drunk was on in the hospital. Lots of my support team and others had committed their weekend to this event. Some came to pray in another room, some brought drinks and food; some came prepared to stay overnight. What commitment! What stars they proved to be!

Alters were triggered almost as soon as the session began. "Carol", an alter who was created to impress the abusers the only way she knew how, by removing her clothes, was the first on the scene once everyone had gathered. Quick as a flash she pulled her trousers and underwear down past her knees before the women present rushed to rescue the situation and preserve my decency. Christopher was on hand to give the sleep signal and, in an unconscious state of deep sleep, I was lifted onto the gurney. Leather straps secured my wrists, ankles, calves, thighs, chest and forehead. The very aggressive alter "Guardian" violently opposed the restraints. She shouted that she hated them all. Eventually Pete managed to engage her in conversation and she was affirmed and encouraged. At least, she was until the name of Jesus was mentioned, at which she reacted with great force. After a long struggle lasting some hours Guardian was delivered of demons and became calm. The restraints were removed and I had something to eat and drink. My body was bruised and chaffing from the struggle against the restraints.

Five people spent the night at the church with me, but I didn't get much sleep. Alters were coming and going in this highly charged atmosphere. I knew it would all turn out OK but not all the inside children did. All the team present slept on the floor in one room, and at one point Victor, one of the support team, was snoring so loudly that we had to move him to the next room!

Early the next morning an alter escaped and ran down the street with Bruce in hot pursuit – it was probably Meg but I don't remember. Once we were ready to begin again the sleep treatment was employed and I was lifted onto the gurney. Stormie came and told the long-held secret of the "blue flame". Apparently an initiation into satanism required the candidates to pass through a circle of blue-flamed candles on the floor into "the middle". The parts of me that gave assent to this were dedicated satanists, but also lost, angry, betrayed and alone. They, too, needed to know the love and redemption of a Christ who forgives and cleanses. This was such good news for them, once they were quiet enough to listen.

I have vague and disjointed memories about it all. We discovered that day that Guardian had been some kind of high priestess; "Satan" (Stephanie, you may recall) was extremely bitter towards just about everyone in the world, especially towards satanists whom, she says, tricked her. She was given a name and promised power and prestige then let down and betrayed (would we expect any different from the father of lies?). She too was delivered that day. The session ended around 2.30 p.m. in the afternoon. I hadn't felt so exhausted since giving birth to Amy! I was wringing with perspiration and so was the gurney. My hair was matted with much tossing and writhing. As I cooled off I got so cold even a blanket couldn't warm me. I felt sick, tense, confused and depressed. People spoke in hushed tones and most went off to find some refreshment while I rested. I remember my stomach feeling really empty but being too exhausted to eat anything. Someone stayed with me and others stood just outside the door, just to be near me. I was given such care and attention. Other support people came and went. Their love was real but for the most part I felt wrung out, unreal, disconnected and terribly, terribly alone.

Meanwhile Christopher was trying to secure a safe place in Mill Creek Hospital, a private and comfortable hospital where I would get the best care. That wasn't to be. The state hospital it was. I cried long and hard at the prospect of having to endure such indignity and harshness again – I had sampled their "care" before. I was so tired and traumatized that all I wanted was to be held and warm and safe.

I was able to face it bravely in the end because of the love and prayers with which I was surrounded. I stayed in the state hospital for two and a half days and then went on to the Mill Creek for a further two and a half days.

After that time the Middle alters made some great turnarounds. "Erica" and Stephanie became particularly strong believers and contributed significantly to my growing sense of stability. Amazingly, the former Middle alters who had become believers were uncompromisingly faithful to Christ. Erica was worrying about the special attention we were getting and our inability to "live like everyone else".

Christopher replied: "But do you think that a person with multiplicity, who's been abused like you have, should necessarily aspire, while they are healing, to live like everybody else? Is that a fair thing?"

"The Bible doesn't give exceptions – the instructions we've been given to live holy lives are the same for everybody, multiple or not."

"OK. It also says there are different parts of the body with different functions; the part of the body that hurts should get attention. I won't excuse bad behaviour but I understand there are reasons we do what we do."

Even JuJu was thinking about the way she acted. One day she commented to Christopher, "I think I'm too much hard work!" I don't know what his reply was, but I suspect he would have silently agreed with her!

I was also becoming more able to look at the bigger picture of our lives set in the context of the kingdom of God: "I want to be radical for God, for I am convinced that I have a job to do, I want to live as one commissioned. But I am frightened, and don't seem to be able to work out what I have to do, or even be able to stay long enough in God's presence to find out. I get restless and agitated sometimes after only five minutes or so... violent tendencies are aroused in me and something happens when I begin to dwell on the things of God."

Chapter
13

Direction

On the outside things were set to change, and for the good. First I was invited to live in the home of a couple in my support group (they were the ones who used to be missionaries in Thailand). We became fast friends; I really loved these people. Lonnie and Elsie were so kind and accepting of the alters. They had eight adult children themselves and I don't know how many grandchildren. Full of wisdom and compassion, their love had clear boundaries and so I felt safe and secure. They also fed me! I ate a full main meal every single day, something that hadn't happened consistently since John and the children had gone. Elsie was such a good cook, we had fresh vegetables each evening, even Brussels sprouts – I was in heaven! On top of that, a dear, elderly couple had heard of my plight and said I could live in the annexe they had next to their house. There was even a work party clearing it all up! Think of that – a whole load of people working away at painting and decorating a place just for me! Al and Bernice were actually choosing to let me live in their own property, and rent-free! It blew my mind. This just had to be God!

On the negative side, I was illegal, and it bothered me. At any point I could be arrested and sent back to England – perish the thought. Lonnie and Elsie had contacted a psychiatrist friend from the University Hospital, Saskatoon, Canada who wrote a letter to the authorities about the importance of my staying in the States to continue in therapy. He writes that being forced to return to England could have serious consequences: "The chance of the alters actually killing Carolyn is a very real possibility... The condition is better understood and much more widely researched in North America than in Britain."

Meanwhile many of the alters were coming to grips with the real world, the world of the present. That posed all kinds of questions, ones that demanded and deserved answers. One day Stephanie had come out in therapy to speak with Christopher.

"Why doesn't God just heal us quickly?" she asked.

"God wants healing but he also wants the truth," he replied.

"But why do we need to come here... why do we need more than God?"

"Relationships with people is part of what is healing."

Stephanie thought for a moment. "Satanists. All they worry about is pleasing Satan. But Christians, they worry about pleasing themselves."

Christopher wasn't stumped at that: "It's OK for Christians to care for themselves. Carolyn is good at giving and helping people but it is OK to look after ourselves too. When Jesus wasn't helping people he was alone, looking after himself emotionally."

She seemed satisfied with that for the time being, but was generally perplexed with what she saw as lethargy in Christians concerning the amazing work of God in Christ, and the lack of vehemence in our proclamation of the gospel. The other alters in the Middle were also slowly learning the truth and became staunch, passionate Christians. They each, in time, integrated – became part of the whole, one person who was me.

At long last we moved into the little annexe we would call home for the next two and a half years. It was beautiful. Newly decorated most tastefully, with flowered curtains and freshly painted walls in matching colours. I was delighted. Al, Bernice and their family became like family to me, and I will be forever grateful to them for their open generosity and welcome. They let me work on their garden, and I planted flowers in the arid Californian soil, watering them religiously twice a day. It paid off, and the garden became a blaze of colour all summer. I was delighted to be able to give something of beauty back to them.

My mother died in November. I was at the church office when the news came, and I felt numb. Pete and the church staff were kind, but it was some days before I could really process what was going on inside. Some of the alters were absolutely adamant that I should not go back for the funeral, though of course my first thought was that I would and should. In my journal I recorded, "Stormie calmly announced that she and others would kill me before we got the chance to reach England." I didn't go.

By the autumn lots of alters were taking an active part in my life, and many feelings and sensations were swirling around my head and body. I struggled, too, with Pete saying he wasn't going to allow us to attend a spiritual warfare conference he was holding at the church. That seemed so unfair. "They just don't understand." I felt cheated and humiliated, like I was some troublemaker who had to be kept away, or a weakling who wouldn't be able to handle the material. Maybe I was both those things in a way, but I didn't mean to be, and felt that I could at least be given the chance. If it didn't work out and things got out of hand, I could always stay away the rest of the time. Anyway, with all my friends there what would I do all week without the people who normally filled my life? Sit alone wishing I were with them? No, it definitely seemed unfair, and I pouted like a sulky teenager. In my journal I wrote:

> Meg is talking about running away, Stormie blames herself for causing Pete's decision, Polly is depressed about it, JuJu thinks we have done something wrong so Pete is cross with us, JC is very angry – and I am disappointed at his lack of trust in me.
>
> "Is it cos he doesn't like us anymore? Is it cos we've done something wrong?" whined JuJu.

We wrote a joint letter to Pete expressing our various views, each alter writing in his or her distinct handwriting (see middle pages for examples). In the end we went!

Christopher had worked very hard at building bridges between the core "me" and the alters, with integration in mind. He was especially keen that we all learn to work together, get to know each other and have shared goals. Sounds crazy – to share a goal with yourself, but I was a divided self, a "double-minded man" as James would have said, "unstable in all he does". I was indeed.

Many of the alters were coming to know the Lord. So a special baptism service took place in the pool in someone's back garden, with all the support team and other friends present. Twenty-three alters were baptised that day, with nine "dunkings" and many of them giving testimony to the way the Lord had delivered us from our occult entrapment. Even though it was still warm in October I was shivering fiercely by the end, both from the cold and the glorious trauma of it all, all recorded on videotape.

JC had decided that at her moment of immersion she would integrate with me though I wasn't sure just what that would mean. When her turn came she stood in the pool and, in her cocky way, gave a moving testimony. She was plunged into the water but when Pete brought her back up there was no one at home! There was no personality present in the body. JC was not there, neither was I. Nor was anyone else! She had obviously gone and nobody had come to take executive control, just a very wet, apparently lifeless body. When I returned I realised that JC had, indeed, integrated with me. Our drive home was hairy. I drove faster and took more risks than I usually did. It was great! There was a wild side to my nature I had not yet discovered. But what fun! I have since very much enjoyed having JC as part of the total me. About November we began to communicate to each other on paper (you can see an example of that in the centre pages).

I desperately missed John and the children whenever I was able to allow myself the painful privilege of thinking about them. Most of the time I didn't dare. The ache inside threatened to crush me, and I couldn't let that happen; I had to keep my head down and plough on with this process of healing. In December I wrote in my journal: "I have a little girl, her name is Amy. When you next see her – you'll know her, she's the most beautiful child there – will you tell her I love her?"

Another time I wrote:

Will there ever be a day when my daughter will want to be like her mum? Will my son ever be as proud of me as I am of him? Will I ever be able to stand in a group of hurting people without the fear that their pain will cause me to flee, and someone else take my place? Will I ever be able to give out of my strength without also taking from my weakness? I have to believe the answer to all these is "yes". YES. Not because I'm in therapy. Not because I'm in this church. Not because I'm in America. But because I'm in Christ – and he has put me where I am today. So, buck up,

Carolyn. Things are looking good. Today was good and the Son of Righteousness comes with healing in his wings.

Charlotte had integrated which meant that "My brain is working more rapidly and profoundly than before – it makes me tired but pretty impressed with my own wisdom!" I realized soon after her integration that she had passed on to me a most valuable gift – I couldn't use a typewriter before, but I found I could now type efficiently, using all my fingers! It appears that each part can develop abilities that should belong to the whole self. Wow, there are advantages to this integration lark after all! Perhaps I will discover other good things about myself when others choose to join with me!

Anyway, therapy progressed in all its terror and wonder. Alters came and went during our twice weekly sessions with Christopher – a new one would be spoken of by a "level one" alter (the most complete and bold alters) then appear one day in the midst of some crisis or other, come and flash their memory or emotion, sweat it out with Christopher, then become integrated. That might happen over days, weeks or months, but it did happen, and fairly often.

Ah! Integration. What a strange and awesome experience that was! One day another part of me would be loud in my mind, pricking fiercely at my tender spots with their gift of memory or feeling, and the next, having discharged their burden, they would be melting willingly into the core that was me, and I would feel strangely whole. Sometimes a little wilder or a little more sensitive, but more "me". Weird? No, completely logical and awesome. Of God. I was becoming well.

However, JuJu and many of the other children were extremely alarmed at the idea of integrating with me. It meant them "going away somewhere" and having to be me and not them. One day Christopher spent a whole session trying to explain to everyone on the inside about integration. It was quite some task, with switches and questions mid-flow. JuJu found all kinds of reasons for not joining with me, "I don't want to go away... I'm JuJu."

"I know you are."

"An' then you will want me to be somebody else."

"It doesn't work that way, it doesn't work that way, JuJu."

"But then I wouldn't play with Maisie any more."

"Well, you'd probably do it with everyone. Together."

"And... would I still hold your hand?"

"If you hold my hand it would probably be together, with everyone. It will be a little different but, you know what, it's not going to be something I tell you that you have to do, OK?"

"But, I don't want to do it."

"All right, that's fine. I'm not going to force you to, OK? But let's just work together, all right?"

"And would I have to wear glasses? I'm not very good at glasses... And I'm not very good at driving the car... And she has to clean the toilet and I don't want to clean the toilet. I don't like cleaning toilets. And I don't like cauliflower!"

"As you work with me I think you'll find these are OK things."

"Would you still like me?"

"I'd still like you, JuJu, whatever happens."

"Even when you're married, would you still like me?"

"You bet."

"Will you like me for ever and ever amen?"

"I'm sure I will always like you, JuJu."

Christopher was trying hard to have Cherub come to speak with him, but JuJu remained out, determined to have her say.

"I keep falling over and I've got two bruises on top of one another. It just looks like one bruise but actually it's two."

"Well, I understand, do the best you can. Sometimes I fall down... Would Cherub..."

"Do you fall down?"

"Well, I trip, OK?"

"Do you get bruises here?" (she points to her knee).

"Once in while. But do your best. Now, does Cherub want to come?" JuJu nods but continues anyway...

"Cherub came out the 'nother day and had a jam sandwich. But she got it all over here," she plasters her hand all over her cheeks.

"That sometimes happens with jam sandwiches. Now, is Cherub ready to come?"

"And I don't have to talk about anything else today?"

"No, we just talked about integration, didn't we. Now, Cherub..."

Eventually JuJu went, most reluctantly, and Cherub came out with definite views about integration.

"I like my name and I don't like the name of Carolyn... what Carolyn does, will I have to do it?... Would Carolyn still like jam sandwiches so that I could have them?"

"I'm pretty sure she'll like them."

Still not sure, Cherub continued, "I don't think the little children [on the inside] would like to hear about it very much, because it's not all that very good, is it?"

"Oh, it's very good. You would be stronger and that's a good thing."

"Would we have to tell the stories before we do it?"

"Yes, you would. It's rather like those streams with the boulders in it. You have to take the boulders out before the separate streams can become one stream."

However, some alters were choosing to integrate. At one

point ten children integrated with me: "Sunshine", "Red", "Destiny", "Noddy", "Blue", "Poppet", "Pippa", "Chipper", "Elizabeth" and "Penny". JuJu, as always, had comments to make: "The little children have gone away into Carolyn 'cept they haven't really gone away, have they?" She was beginning to get hold of the right idea.

Some of the alters were amazingly different from who I knew myself to be. For example, JuJu had 20-20 vision and yet I was very short-sighted. One day we went to the optician to check on my glasses. At some point during my eye test JuJu must have come out. The optician was mystified: "How come you are able to read this line, when the strength of your spectacles among other things tell me you shouldn't be able to?" I tried to explain dissociation and he was further intrigued. He did some more tests, and invited me to return later in the week, out of hours, to examine my sight some more. But I didn't go. It seemed to some of the alters a little too close to being discovered. And anyway, there were more pressing things to pay attention to at that time than satisfying one man's curiosity – but his findings might have been interesting!

I had one alter who was unable to walk, and shuffled along the ground on her stomach. One time I was caught in a sudden thunderstorm as I crossed the Campus after a therapy session, and this alter was immediately triggered by the thunder and lightening, "came out" and I dropped to the ground like a piece of rag. She crawled to the safety of the reception building using her elbows to drag herself along, and the forever-kind receptionist helped her into an office to wait for Christopher to be free to attend to her. Though I was soaked through I wasn't able to come back and dry myself down for about two hours, as this alter stayed out and immobile.

Another alter, "Millie", continually wailed pathetically, "Will somebody help me? Will somebody help me?" That is what she had wanted so desperately to say when bad things were happening, long ago, but was unable to.

"Whisper" only spoke in hushed tones for fear of attracting dangerous attention, and "Panda" was a large, heavy-set, aggressive young male! His name arose from the fact that he wore only black and white and rather resembled a night-club "bouncer". Each alter was created for a reason and with a purpose. It all made perfect sense when you consider the trauma from which each was created.

It was therefore not surprising that experiencing the people inside sometimes became overwhelming.

> I hurt. A hundred years of pain and loneliness rests on my shoulders. I am crushed. It has been too long; there has been too much darkness; sometimes the fire inside me has been all but extinguished. They don't understand. The people. The people who try to understand, who try to reach out, never quite reach far enough. They never quite get there. It's too far to go, too deep, too dark, altogether too painful. Only I can taste its bitterness.
>
> I have been hurt, I know I have. How can I express the wound, the damage, the injustice? How can I show you, tell you, convey to you what it's like? There is forever a jagged cut from my head to my feet that refuses to heal. I am torn in two, with only temporary relief. Those things should not have happened. *They should not have happened. God why did you let them happen? It's broken me.* Will I ever be put together again? Will I ever be free of pain? Will I ever cease to hurt?
>
> O God. Please help me!

My writing often didn't seem to make any sense, but I was trying my hardest to bring some order out of what appeared to be chaos. It wasn't, of course – chaos, that is. As with all people with MPD, my very well-organized inner system kept me functioning amazingly well. Each alter had a place and a role, but sometimes they were at odds with me and with each other and when I tried to explain it on paper it didn't sound right:

I want to be violent. I want to cut. I want to smash things. I feel like I want to go mad. But I want to be touched. I wish someone were here to hug me, cover me, protect me. *No – don't get near me.* I don't know what to do, I don't know what to do, I don't know what to do… I want to explode and let the others out loose once and for all. It's all so veiled and enigmatic. The unknown and the vaguely known are scary. It's too dim and confusing to see from where I am standing… it's all moving too fast, it's too crowded. JuJu is too open, she's too words. She's small and yet way too big, too close. Somebody has a runny nose.

It took real teamwork to keep me alive and functioning, but God was supplying all my needs. One day Heide took me to a grocery store to spend money supplied by my good friends, Bruce and Susan, and I wrote in my journal: "It is such a good feeling to choose my own food." After that I was given money every month for groceries. Others had me to their home regularly for meals, or took me out, or invited me to swim in their pool. Lonnie got hold of a car for my use, and filled it weekly with petrol for me; others took me out for breakfast and sometimes even to the coast for a trip out. Someone bought me some new clothes. What gems they were for me! I was beginning to really taste what it could be like to live outside of the confines of my depression and intense mental struggles, and I liked it. It forever amazed me that each person in my support team, all so different and miles away from being counsellors or professionals, would choose to stick around. I was from another culture. I spoke of things completely outside their world experience or understanding. But they loved, and kept on loving.

They gave me a surprise birthday party and showered gifts on me: English food items from Cosco, a watering can for my gardening attempts, and so much more. How kind. Their laughter at the guileless honesty of my child parts, and their genuine compassion at the inner pain other alters described, was a vital part of my healing. I was beginning to believe that I was OK. That maybe I could be good enough on occasion, that just maybe there was something in my heart that could be lovable.

As I became more functional I began to look for useful things to do apart from the "getting better" that had been the be all and end all up until then. I was thrilled to be given a role: some counselling in the church. Pete gave me a little office and I saw those who were struggling with all the stuff that surrounds early trauma. In fact, I started to counsel those with MPD! I had a small case load, my own phone, and felt like the bees knees. I was needed. There was a place for me. I was being a very good girl and tried with every fibre of my being to be the very best counsellor the world had ever seen. I wasn't! Although the incredibly resourceful and creative women I saw in the counselling room made significant progress, they did not get completely better. None of them stopped being MPD over the year I was counselling them. But I learnt so much through them.

I was in a ponderous mood during these days, wondering what the next step should be. Crisis was no longer a daily experience; neither was panic my automatic reaction to the unknown. It was time to face my responsibilities, such a frightening concept. It meant preparing for the day that I tear myself away from the cosy embrace of my support group and flex my own emotional muscles.

I mustn't be afraid. But I am. Yes, I am. Alone, afraid, but with the skills I am learning, the deep relationships I have made and the precious gift God gave me in Christopher, it will all be OK. I have so much, so many memories of love and care and compassion. Have learnt so much about myself and others in Christopher's consistent and unchanging counsel, his belief in me, his loyalty, his godly advice. I am rich with the things no one can take from me.

The Lord continued to provide for my needs. One day Becky rang Elsie in tears. We were working hard at counselling and helping others and Becky couldn't understand why other people got paid for their work and we didn't. Elsie patiently explained that it is the Lord's approval that really matters, but Becky was unconsoled: "But that doesn't buy us trainers", she sobbed. That evening I went to a meeting and was met with friends bearing two bags of groceries and a brand-new pair of trainers!

It was the strength I gained from this kind of love that enabled me to give something away. I started a support group for women who had MPD. At one point I decided to take them to the mountains for a few days. Michelle, from my own support group, and I drove them up to a log cabin high in the heavily forested mountainside of the Sierras. What an adventure! Four women with multiple personalities, including me, and one "normal" person, Michelle. The idea was that we went to get away from it all. I'm not sure we got away from anything; in fact it was quite the reverse!

Right from the start they were all switching freely; there were alters coming and going all over the place! It was like looking after a house full of small children. Strangely all three of the other multiples had alters who spoke using sign language, which meant that they would communicate with each other in a way that excluded Michelle or me at times. Slightly unnerving!

Going for a walk in the forest was something else! All three of them had been abused in a satanic ritual setting and were easily triggered, we were soon to discover, by lonely, natural environments. Like a forest, for instance. One lady, small, plump and with a very fragile personality, kept switching to a child who believed she had ants crawling over her. We only had to spot a creepy crawly on the forest floor when out came a distressed child who needed to be pacified and some firm reality checks applied. The whole experience would have been a hoot had it not been for the fact, never far from our minds, that their fragmentation was the result of horrific abuse. Nevertheless we had a lot of fun together, explored the countryside and learnt about ourselves.

Were we completely crazy to have attempted that? I don't think so. We wanted to bring some normality, if not light-hearted fun, to a few women whose lives were blighted with pain and dividedness. It was all we knew how to do. So we did it. I learnt about setting firm boundaries, and not giving in to every expressed fear or perceived need. I did what Christopher had done for me, and felt that in some small way I was giving something back.

In August I spent some time at Hume Lake in the Kings Canyon National Park, taking time out to think through where I was going. My children came alive in every youngster I saw in that holiday environment.

I think often of my children. Each time I watch a little boy, barefoot, awkward, maybe 8 or 9-years-old, I think of Luke. Peering into every hole and rock crevice, loudly sharing his findings with his friends scattered on the rocks; jumping daringly from each small rise onto the rock below, trying his utmost to show his friends how unafraid he is – tongue out, concentrated frown, employing every ounce of courage he possesses.

I can just imagine Lukey being among them: full of life and energy, and the unsinkable optimism God graced him with from birth. Brimming with questions and suggested answers, with ideas and plans and projects. Thinking no further ahead than the next step in the plot, the next adventure when this one is over. Dear Luke, fair head, streaked bronze when the light hits it a certain way, eagerly bobbing up and down as he runs to be the first to make a serious discovery.

I see my little boy in every eight-year-old explorer I pass as I walk around the lake. But he isn't here. He is six-and-a-half thousand miles away, playing with mothers' sons I haven't met, going to a school I haven't visited, living in a home I haven't cared for. My heart is like lead.

And there is Amy. Now quite a little lady no doubt, as she approaches eleven-years-old. Her long brown hair always was so pretty, giving her a strikingly petite, almost cameo appearance. The girls I pass on my solitary wandering are food for my musings and imagination. How tall is my little girl now? Are her legs as slim as that one's, or taking on some shapely feminine form as that one? Does she chatter loudly in a large group, or prefer to have one dear friend to deeply confide in? Are her movements still so very quick and sprightly or has maturity introduced some elegancy and steadiness into her actions? Has her impetuosity been tempered or will that trait characterize her for ever?

Beautiful young girls pass me, intent in their conversation. Amy is not with them. My eyes search in vain among the long brown locks. Stop looking, Carolyn, you will not find her here.

You're usually unaware of being in a rut until your knee bumps the side of the groove and you realize you are hemmed in. It was while I was at Hume Lake that my knees did the bumping. Oh my gosh! I'm jogging along in a comfortable furrow and I'm not even sure I'm heading in the right direction. Time for some digging – a new track is called for, one that leads me back to my husband and children. Not that life could honestly be called "comfortable". Bearable, perhaps. In some areas it was almost approaching normal. But having dozens of insiders speaking their mind, not to mention the whole income business – dependent on others and all – life could never be comfortable.

But it was now time to strike out away from the safety I had earnestly sought with tears and had found with such relief. As soon as the pressure eased, as soon as I could relax a bit at last, things had to change, become dangerous again. I wanted it safe, predictable, without risk. I wanted God to be safe, but that can never be. As CS Lewis wrote about Aslan in the Narnia stories: "Safe? Who said anything about safe? 'Course he isn't safe. But he's good." God is good. That's what I could hold onto. And it was enough.

Chapter
14

Decision

At any point in our healing journey, that long and arduous tramp into dangerous territory, it would be quite tempting to set up camp at a sheltered spot, fed up with the constant changes and challenges. We would like to fit a carpet in our tent, plug in a telly and settle down. "Enough of this tiring plod, healed or not, I'm not budging." But without the adventure and the moving on, we won't grow what it takes in our hearts to see and recognize the celestial city. We won't know when to rejoice, to leap and dance at the presence of the good shepherd. We will still be in front of the "box", stagnating, growing old and bitter. I want to grow in my freedom and maturity, danger or no, pain or no. Stagnation is not on my agenda.

It was decided, by a process of osmosis I suppose, that it was right to disband the support group. It was quite true that I didn't need the members in the same way that I had once. I was now stable, no longer in crisis. Healing and integration were routine; I had friends, a home and a role. I felt I belonged, and I was moving forward. Some of the alters, of course, had some difficulty with the group going. At least, JuJu did ("Have I done something wrong? Don't they like me any more? An' then, will they hurt me?"), and those behind her. But then things began to get a bit messy. Relationships. Somehow I had become unpopular with some of the support group members, but I still don't understand why or what caused the ill feelings. It remains a somewhat painful mystery; but then, change never has been popular, or easy.

The support group had done so well; the cavalry had boldly and sacrificially ridden in and rescued the victim. Now she was herself riding on horseback, sword in hand, and our valiant fighters were left a little disoriented. I have a feeling I might have stopped being so grateful, or at least, verbalizing it. I'm not sure though, it's just a hunch, as I honestly did, and still do, feel extremely grateful for all my friends who gave so much so willingly. I certainly would never in a million years have intended them to feel taken for granted.

Anyway, things were changing. The shift in emotions sent me to my knees. "Who am I now if I wasn't 'poor little Carolyn', fragmented, lost, alone? Who am I Lord? How do I live? Where do I live? I don't know what to do – what happens now? I must come to grips with these questions. Yes, of course, of course, I am a child of God. A wife. A mother. What do I do now?" In my journal I wrote:

Oh! Where am I heading? Shouldn't I be ready to return to John and stop such foolishness? All the older people in my life are praying furiously for our reuniting as a family. That is, of course, the right thing. How scary that is, and yet I grieve daily for my dear children. How stupid I am – and confused – and scared... I feel like a child again... Help me, Lord! Please hear my cry and rescue me!

This has to be the beginning of "make your mind up time". I was still writing to John and the children each week. John was still replying though the children's precious little notes and messages were not so frequent. The pressure both inside and out was on – was it time to prepare to return to England?

People around me were making it plain that they thought so. It seemed as though my friends were turning against me. Was I paranoid? Were they actually now tired of me? Or perhaps I really had done something wrong; maybe I was not a good girl after all; I had been bad all along and was just kidding myself that I was OK. I tried hard to discern where the unpleasant vibes were coming from and why they were there. I felt very uncomfortable and my suspicions were confirmed when I went to see Pete. He told me he felt that I "outgrew him" a long time ago. This wasn't supposed to happen, people were not supposed to drift away from me. I don't know how to handle rejection other than "going away" into another alter, but I was learning not to do that, but rather to face the pain. All the same, I thought, I'm not ready for this.

Then there was the disturbing call home. I rang Amy on her birthday – a wonderful conversation with her rattling on happily about home and school. But John was bland and distant. His comment on my idea of joining him in England was "Oh no, I don't think that'll work."

"No tender explanation, or sign of gratitude or joy that I am thinking about our reunion. I feel angry," I wrote in my journal.

The anxiety that began in my mind and body at returning to England was revving up. Supposing nobody really wants me home after all. Perhaps my family really had decided to reject me. Can I bear to be alone? How would the alters cope? Would they kill me? Would I face rejection from everybody?

I feel as though a heavy weight has been tied to my chest and I am destined to carry it for ever. The pit of my stomach is continually nauseous, with butterflies bouncing from there to my heart, which has taken to pounding loudly at irregular intervals. My throat and jaws feel tight, constricted, as though set to face something bad and painful. Facing the dentist, be it for a complete detoothing, could never be as bad as this… I feel as traumatized as if eyeball to eyeball with a great disaster. I am braced and ready for the attack.

But plans had to be made, that was now plain. A friend who took me grocery shopping each month suddenly said she felt God wanted me to go back to England and so was not prepared to help me out in that way beyond Christmas. Then I received a wonderful but traumatizing gift in the post – photographs of my children. I had been longing to see their photographs for so many months, and begging John to send some. He never did. Why? I was later to learn that his coldness, and lack of enthusiasm for my return, was simply a reflection of his desperation not to be let down or disappointed. He had sunk beyond any hope that I would go back and in his anger and hopelessness saw only false hopes. But to me it felt as though I was no longer wanted. I was sure, however, that my children would need me.

They have grown so much, they look (in the photos) so brave, so valiant; seeing them evoked such strange and deep emotions in me. So very, very deep; a great longing for them, even greater than I have yet experienced, which has been heart wrenching enough. A longing to be their mother, to talk with them, learn with them. Help Amy make choices about her dress and her looks. Help Luke to be assertive and believe in himself; help them to be all that God made them to be. I want to clothe them and trim their hair, make their home cosy and welcoming, feed them with good things, give them a role model, a mother they can be proud of.

Lukey used to be so pleased to hold my hand and walk down the road. When he showed me his paintings his little chest would swell so, he was proud to present his efforts to his mum. Amy used to watch me and follow me and copy me. My habits and ways became hers. She looked after her dolls the way I looked after little Luke. In staying here in America I robbed them of all of that. Yes, I was busy fighting for survival, but they didn't understand that. They just knew that mummy wasn't with them any more, she stayed behind. And the long wait for her to come home began ...

Then my mind wondered, as it often did, to myself as a child:

When you're a child you try so very hard to be good, to do the right thing, and yet you're never quite sure you made it. All the time you're looking for some small indicator that you did OK, that you weren't a nuisance, that you didn't mess things up for everyone else. But always there lurked that nagging, gnawing suspicion that you've got it wrong again...

I missed out. I got left behind... It feels as though so much of my life has been spent waiting. Waiting for someone to run back and get me. Because I didn't know the way. I was too small to go it alone, but nobody noticed. No one came... Now my children wait. What have I done to them?

How my heart hurts. So very, very badly. I think I am going to break and my mind will get lost in the debris. I know I was a little girl once. I don't really remember, I just know. But I was lost, and I waited and waited, and nobody came. I didn't matter. I just do it wrong. It takes a long time to get strong when you know you are weak and small and ugly, and disposable. It's so nice to feel useful. I think I was glad they used me. I still want to be useful and helpful so that people are glad that I'm there, and notice me and won't want to leave me behind. I really don't want to be left behind. I really don't want to be lost or ignored... Am I doing it wrong? Please tell me I'm doing OK. Please.

The number of alters, including those who had already integrated, had risen to an astonishing 109 which was to be the final total as far as I am aware. Many, however, had gone, become part of me or another alter – but I was still not whole. There was still work to do. I felt as though I could spend the rest of my life listening to the poison of the abuse, and still not hear it all. I determined that I had heard enough, though. I now knew the kind of things that took place. Surely I could put the rest behind me? Surely the remaining alters could simply melt into the background and I could pick up the tattered shreds of my life and make a new start?

I spoke with Christopher in earnest about preparing to return to England. This *must* be my last Christmas without my family. This *must* be the last time the children wake up on Christmas morning with no mummy to gather up the wrapping paper or kiss her "thank yous" for the gifts they have given. Next year I will, *I will*, be with them when they open the little surprises I have prepared for each day of Advent; when they unpack their stockings on Christmas morning; when they find the coin in their Christmas pudding. I began to prepare my mind for my return. I watched a video of Queen Elizabeth and wrote: "I could almost believe that God is British! I can feel the stirrings of pride within me that I have such a heritage of quality, style and excellence. The British traditions are rich and meaningful…I am English and always shall be."

I also had to tackle another issue – it felt increasingly, as I became more whole, that I had made it all up, and that I was a phoney. I had to come to some place of acceptance. If I made it all up, then I am an unspeakably evil person, leading so many wonderfully accepting, intelligent people astray. What a scheming mind I must have. That knowledge will be hard to live with. But harder still is the thought that perhaps, just perhaps, it is all true; that I really was horribly, ritualistically abused in a satanic setting, over and over again, and as a result my mind fragmented. The implications of that are completely overwhelming. It was *me, my* body, that they did those things to. No. I would rather believe I am an evil and deceitful person. At least then I can change, and say sorry, and live a better life from now on.

It is now recognized that dissociation is a way of forgetting, for a time. The mind siphons off the bad memories into a separate part, and reclaiming those hidden-away memories is a complex process. So, when the memories resurface it does not feel as though they belong to you, it feels alien, more as if someone had told them to you, or you had seen the images in a film.

I struggled to think it through on paper, in my journal:

I must accept that I have MPD; and that, as a result of SRA. It seems that a leap of faith is in order here – I do not feel like a multiple (though how do I know what it feels like to be one if I've only ever been me and nothing else?!). The people who assure me that I am are, annoyingly, people I trust and respect – and I can readily believe them in every other area. So I will determine to believe them. I will. I will. I have multiple personality disorder. That is who I am.

I was abused. As a small child. I was badly hurt. Somebody hurt me. Lots of people hurt me when I was little. Very little. It felt like it does in my dreams. I didn't want to be there. But I was small and young and I had no choice. When I think of these things I don't remember anything but I do have screams in my head, and a dark sensation, dark and dark green. I think it must have been very bad. Lots and lots of it. Over and over and over. It feels like if I ever really felt it again I would die, I would just shrivel up. It happened over and over again. On and on and on and on.

And there were dark feelings. Not just outside feelings, or inside feelings, but beyond feelings. Bad ones. Satanic ritual abuse is what my alters describe. Bad people doing bad things.

And I was there. And they hurt me in their happenings. On and on and on and on.

I really did know what the truth was. And I didn't like it one bit. Either way I had to face an uncertain future.

Once I had made the decision to return, the stark realization hit that I would be returning to the land in which I was abused. I looked at more videos about England and its beautiful countryside but felt only the sickly heaviness of fear.

Would I be in danger if I returned to England? I wasn't supposed to tell; I would be punished if I did. Was that true? Had I been believing a lie, a myth? Would I face reprisals if I returned? Would my family suffer? What would happen to my children if the bad people found out where we lived?

By the end of the month I had decided to leave the church that had shown me such love and given me such hope. There seemed to no longer be a place for me there. I had clearly offended people, but still didn't know what it was I had done. If only someone would be honest and tell me, then I would gladly do all I could to set it right. I had apologized profusely to all and sundry, but still didn't know what for! The decision was a very hard one to make. But my last months in the States needed to be stable in order to muster the courage to return to the "land of terrors". If I remained in the church I would only be putting myself in a position of pain; I really didn't need that. It meant, though, breaking a commitment, and loyalty is important to me.

My usual plan is: if in doubt continue until God has made it very, very plain you are to break that commitment. This was clearly becoming one of those times. However, not all my support network went to the same church; I was still surrounded by caring friends. It was important that each "today" was filled with meaning, and blessing for others. I resolved more than ever before that I would not leave America without having given something to others, as I have received so much myself. I would be deserting many of those people who have given so much to me. So, was I bad for leaving a church? I wanted to be a good girl, and I clearly wasn't one yet.

Life went on. A tutor friend invited me to attend his class in psychotherapy and pastoral counselling at the local seminary. What a challenge! It meant I was a real, ordinary person – sitting in a classroom with other students. We learnt about mental illness, and therapeutic methods. It was an academic exercise to many of the others, but to me it touched so much on what had been happening to me. As I had been seeing clients myself for the last year it seemed altogether expedient to begin to make efforts at formal training. But it was so scary – the "normal person" bit, that is. The academic work I found easy.

I recorded in my journal at that time:

This is a sort of litmus test on what I am capable of, and who I can be if I really tried, and I must not fail. This is a threshold I just have to cross, even if it means sweating and crying and straining every spiritual muscle and mental nerve that I have. I *can* be a person, a real person, like other people, if I tried hard enough and did not give up. Please, Lord, hear my cry – you know and understand what this means to me. Please make this happen for me and set me free to be a real person.

God answers that kind of prayer so well! I passed all the exams with straight As and felt as though I was catching up on the race to be real.

Once I had decided to return to England the hard bit was knowing how to go about it. I had no money for fares, that was certain. The other thing I was certain was that this was the right thing to do. I was very *un*certain whether John wanted me back. I had been receiving mixed messages from him. On the one hand he had been saying for months, years: when are you coming home? On the other he was knocking down flat every plan and idea I had of actually doing that. I was also pretty sure that his family would be antagonistic towards me; things had never been very easy in relationships there. And as for my side of the family – I hadn't heard from anyone at all, not even my sister, so assumed they were all very angry with me and would not want to know me. As is turned out my sister, Kate, had no idea what was going on, and left it to John to let her know.

I hoped to return in April, so I had asked John to help me put two things in place before I did. First, could he perhaps find some nearby accommodation I could stay in for a week or two until the children got used to my being around? My plan was to be in the home during the day but sleep elsewhere so that at first I was the visiting mummy; they would then have time to build up a relationship with me. Suddenly foisting myself upon them sounded demanding and unfair for them. I also asked if he could help me find a therapist in England to whom I could go once I was back. I tried to do that myself, but it was difficult given that I was so far away. I didn't have a clue about such things – when I lived in England I had never heard of therapists or counselling.

Neither of those things happened; no accommodation was found, nor a counsellor, therefore I didn't make the journey in April. John was disgusted: "See, I knew you wouldn't come." I felt frustrated and confused: does he want me or not? Should I go anyway and risk rejection? Perhaps I must just try to prove that I really want to do this. I decided to take the bull by the horns and go back anyway, home or no home; therapy or no therapy. I had received so much here in this foreign land. I had discovered why I was the way I was, I had found a depth of friendship and understanding I had never dreamt was possible. I had been loved and heard. I had also been in the mental wards of three different hospitals over seven different admissions; I had been betrayed, abandoned and misunderstood. It was time to go.

Then began the round of yard sales and speaking engagements to help raise money. People were generous and helpful and eventually I had enough funds to fly me, together with six large boxes of accumulated possessions and lots of presents for John and the children, back to dreaded England. Two days before I was due to fly out of San Francisco I spoke at a church service. I still needed $375 to complete the fee for my extra baggage but only my close friends knew that. At the end of my talk the pastor, someone I didn't know, stood and said he felt the Lord nudging him to take up an offering for me. There was simply a basket left at the back for anyone to give if they chose to. It was not a large church, maybe sixty or seventy people were present that evening. Over coffee at the end the pastor came up to me; he had counted the money in the basket – $375!

God had proved himself to be the guardian and provider again and again. He would continue to supply my every need in England – but what would I find when I got there? Would John be happy to see me? Would the children reject me? What about their caring church family who had helped John look after the children while he was at work? Would they open their arms and hearts to me? I was sure they would, and looked forward to being embraced as the long-lost missing part of the family. I was soon to be sadly disillusioned.

Saying goodbye to all the people who had become real family to me was so painful. I may never see them again. Promises of letters sounded hollow and unreliable. Altogether

I had four farewell parties and any number of treats and gifts. A whole crowd of people travelled to San Francisco airport to see me off the day of my departure. I had a wide group of friends by this time and so some of the folks that travelled with us in Viv's large people-carrier didn't know each other. It was a heart-wrenching event, one that will be etched in my memory for ever. I wore a deep pink trouser suit that Al and Bernice had bought me for the event – I have it still. But etched far deeper in my memory is the sight of my darling children waiting for me, after three-and-a-half years, at the other end of my journey.

Part 3

Chapter
15

Reunion

My heart was thumping as hard as my loaded trolley as it bumped over the lumpy airport floor. Feeling dry-mouthed and weak I made my entrance through the barriers with trepidation. Who will be there? Will they recognize me? Where are they? I scanned the sea of faces peering out towards the emerging passengers, ruffled and worn after the eleven-hour flight. Then I caught a glimpse of dad in the mass. After that everything happened so fast. A little boy broke out from the crowd and ducked under the barriers. He was in my arms before I knew what was happening. My Lukey. My darling, wonderful Luke. I held him as though I would never, could never, ever let him go. He had grown so much, what a big, strong, beautiful boy he was. Then came Amy. A glorious, marvellous, magical moment. Her arms hugged me tight, and I was in heaven. My lovely little girl was in my arms at last, I could feel her warmth for real, this was not just a dream. I was with them again. The Hallelujah chorus had struck up, the trumpets were sounding – we are together again! Oh wonderful, wonderful day!

John's embrace was not so certain, but real enough. He was as unsure about this as I, though he and dad were obviously pleased to see me. I realized, in my groggy, jet-lagged way, that I had work to do; but that was to come. For the moment I was home, whatever that meant.

My sister, Kate had also taken the trouble to meet me there at the airport. It was good to see her again – such a relief to know she was still happy to call me "sister" and to go out of her way to meet me even though I had shut her out of my life for so long. Between us we managed to heave all the boxes into waiting cars. We all made the long, grey, winding journey through driving rain and low, black, British clouds to my new home.

I thought it would be tough but I had never imagined it would be this tough. The church did not embrace and welcome me, in fact they were cold and suspicious. Assuming they would like me I at first acted as though they were happy to see me. Looking back I feel only acute embarrassment at my confidence. That confidence soon ebbed away in the increasing realization that my presence provoked anger and indignation. Of course, why would they welcome someone who had, apparently, abandoned her husband and small children in some selfish pursuit? They didn't know or understand what was going on with me, and felt only protective defensiveness on my family's behalf. I honour them for their love and loyalty towards John, Amy and Luke. In the end I chose not to attend church at all rather than face sitting alone, for try as I might, conversation with church members was a forced and farcical affair. I always seemed to say the wrong thing and make a fool of myself. It was plain I was not liked, and I felt frustrated that I was never really given the chance to prove my worth; nevertheless I can see things from their viewpoint. They were a caring community and their hearts were right.

That wasn't the only thing that isolated me. Neither John's nor my wider family were happy with me, in fact everyone was positively stony-faced and cool. After all, I had chosen to look after myself rather than care for my family. Kate was unsure of how to approach me, so stayed quietly in the background. Our occasional telephone conversations stayed on trivial matters. Some thought I had got caught up in a weird Californian cult. I dare not think about what others thought I was up to. But most didn't know the truth, so why would, should they believe any different? On the other hand, they could have chosen to trust me; given me the benefit of the doubt. My grief was raw and piercing.

John went back to full-time work, but I hadn't had to shop, cook or clean for a family for three-and-a-half years, and now, having moved straight into the family home, I was thrown into that role with no rehearsal time at all. We had no car so I had to walk long distances to the supermarket, or catch a bus which we could seldom afford. But I threw myself into trying to be the very best wife and mother there was, picking up from where I had left off. It was all so very new; a completely different area of the country from the northern town we had lived in before moving to the States, and extremely unlike the hot, dusty, wide Californian town with its laid-back, all-accepting mood. Would I be able to stick it out?

My days were filled with housework: there was much sorting, cleaning, tidying, arranging and repainting to be done. The house needed a woman's touch: some flowers here, an ornament there, a display of the children's artwork could adorn this door, and a box for their toys could fit in this corner. I wanted to be sure it was squeaky clean for my little ones and husband. At last I felt the flat was as pleasant and welcoming as I could make it, given so few resources. John and the children bore my rearrangements with great grace. Their home was suddenly changed; all of us had to endure a great deal of alteration and upheaval, and each coped as best they could. But the changes hurt.

We lived in an upstairs flat above a bustlingly busy pet shop along a noisy road, next door to a pub. The constant groan of slow-moving vehicles past our window gnawed at my jagged nerves. In addition there was the sound of the parrots squawking and the customers parking, the shoppers gossiping and the drinkers laughing. I hate noise, and so hated this place. There was no garden to provide me with escape or a healthy space for the children. That, at least, was a challenge I could rise to.

There was a square of concrete balcony outside our back door, our only door as a matter of fact; it was surrounded by a waist-high brick wall, just right for pots and tubs to stand on. The charity shop down the road had all manner of interesting containers on its shelves, so for few pence we soon had a garden. There were flowering plants in great abandon by the summer – in an old leather boot, overflowing the inside of a clapped-out chip pan fastened to the wall, in old broken buckets, in new ninety-nine pence plastic buckets, in large pots, in old pots, in small pots. I watered them every day and fed them religiously. Never was such old junk treated with such affection – they housed my new babies, and they did me proud. By the end of the summer we had seen a glorious riot of red and blue, purple and yellow, flowing and creeping and spilling onto the grey concrete, creating an oasis of colour and life. Every corner throbbed with gaiety and provided some hope that things in my inner life could change. If I sow the right seed, the harvest will surely come.

Still I ached for safety but God provided bright spots, like stars in a night sky. I jumped from star to star across the blackness, and was led in the right direction. One such star was Judy, my new, long-sought-after counsellor. Cheerful, kind, unbending, firm, reliable Judy. I was infuriated by her refusal to be swayed by my emotions. She would not show sympathy for my dreadful plight, nor would she in any way re-enforce my self-pity. The things going on in my life just were, that's all, and there will be a way through.

As she listened to me I listened to myself. I heard myself whining with self-pity and I also heard myself being strong, full of faith and joy. I learnt much. God began to teach me the lesson, now just a faint realization but later to be a delicious revelation, that I could choose. I could choose to be strong or I could choose to be stubborn, desperate, childish. I could let go and just let JuJu take over, stuttering hysterically, talking herself into a frenzy; I could let other alters come and sully my mind with sad, bad memories. Or I could focus on all that is good and true. Ultimately it was my choice, those alters were still me.

Judy simply sat and calmly absorbed it all. She was my safe place, I was accepted and heard when no one else, it seemed, was able or willing to embrace who I was, warts – and alters – and all. Judy hadn't worked with alters before and though I felt slightly responsible for her "education" I never felt one whiff of judgment or rejection. She was willing to learn and provided a sense of security in a very insecure situation. The fortnightly meetings gave me a time to spill my anger and grief, and restore some backbone to my wobbly sense of self. She provided the line upon which I could peg the laundry of my broken life. I could look at it and see that though it was now clean my life was still in tatters. I appreciated her strength and acceptance. Gradually I was able to tell her something of my story.

Seeing Judy was, however, costly. Not that she overcharged me, not at all, but I had no means of transport. I couldn't drive in the UK and, anyway, we couldn't afford to buy or run a car. That meant I had to make the fortnightly trip to the next village by shank's pony. I usually found it a painful challenge to climb the steps up to our flat, or walking at all sometimes, so making the thirty-five minute trek on foot to see Judy was often excruciatingly exhausting. My whole body would hurt for days afterwards. It was usually the only trip out I made all week. Looking back I wonder how I managed it. Another God thing I suppose.

Before I found Judy I had a brief spell with a psychiatrist in London who found me interesting, but who forbade me ever to dissociate in his presence. The restrictions and implied rejection of who I was increased a sense of grief that was hard to bear. I didn't stay with him for long.

I had begun to write about ritual abuse, and a series of articles was published in a well-known Christian counselling magazine, though I used a pen name. In my research I met a detective called Steve who was also aware of terrible child abuse occurring in British communities. Although I had not intended to, we got talking about my own experiences. He was affirming and helpful as I struggled to apply my adult, objective, analytical mind to the whole issue of ritual child abuse.

I left the Baptist church that John and the children had belonged to and tried the Anglican church in another village. I was invited to join a house-group, and there met some wonderful people. John was not keen at first for he had really gelled with the people in the Baptist church, but he eventually came along too, and for six months, until we moved, I felt that at last we had found some real friends. Hanni and Paul, Bennie and Mark were such good fun, and they genuinely cared; what a relief it was to find that life could be about laughing and joking too.

But the fumes and the noise around our home did nothing to improve a growing weariness and exhaustion. The GP had no explanation for it, as she did not recognize the existence of a condition from which I was convinced I was suffering –

M.E. I experienced all the classic symptoms but as I was unaware of any remedy I had to try as best I could to live with an utter weariness of being. I was awarded Severe Disablement Allowance, having been classified 80 per cent disabled. It hurt even to walk up the stairs, and sometimes I was so weary the task of blinking felt too much. Sometimes at night I would be unable to go to sleep because I felt so very hungry; my whole body felt far too tired to digest anything in the evening. I was too hungry to sleep but too tired to eat. Stalemate.

John was, at his request, transferred in his job as Post Office clerk to a town at the other end of the county. I was relieved even though it meant moving far away from our new friends and from Judy. It was a new start for all of us, a chance to put behind us the disruption of the past few years and begin as a united family in a place where we were unknown. The trouble was – we had no money. How can you buy a house with just one mediocre income and absolutely nothing behind us? We had rented our present flat, draining us of every penny arriving in our bank account. Prayer was, of course, the best, the only, option. So that's what we did.

We came across a "shared ownership" scheme whereby we could effectively rent half a house and buy the other. We immediately put our names on the waiting list and... well, waited. These homes, it turned out, were being renovated, so the waiting had as much to do with builders and planners as with legalities. We rented a house in the next town as a half-way measure while the builders drank tea and had meetings and waited for materials to arrive. It was amazing that we were even allocated one. Apparently we were originally near the bottom of the long list but somehow ended up at the top, even given the astounding privilege of choosing our house! That was a very real miracle.

The day before the intended move we heard from our solicitors that the insurers were refusing our application because of my medical history – they doubtless thought I was one slice short of a sandwich. What should we do? Was the long, stressful wait for our own home, to put down roots and be a "normal" family, the carrot we were never to crunch? We prayed hard and desperately. Once more God resolved the situation and we were accepted at the last moment without the insurance.

The three months we expected to live in temporary accommodation turned into fifteen months, but the great day came when we loaded up the hired van and travelled the ten miles, once more in driving rain, to our new home. On the way we turned a sharp bend in the narrow country lane and were met by the sight of a magnificent and dazzling rainbow, smiling and rippling in the grey sky over the sodden hedge! God had not forgotten us after all.

Around this time our fourteen-year-old daughter developed, quite suddenly and without obvious warning, the gut-wrenching, thieving, life-depriving illness of anorexia nervosa. Her weight plummeted to a mere four-and-a-half stone and our lives as a family were blighted with anxiety and the inner conflict that accompanies the questions: Why is she so unhappy that she wants to starve herself? Our children had always been so content and stable. Should we have done something earlier? How could we have prevented it? Was it our fault? Does that mean we are bad parents? How can we rescue our child from herself? For the next eight years Amy fought and rebelled, spitting her hatred of herself, of the world, of us. It is a spiteful illness that defies rational explanation. Of course I gave of myself, more than I really had to give, to try to bring resolution – talking, reassuring, commanding, pleading… Amy would enter a hospital in-patient eating programme, regain the necessary weight to at least stay alive, come out of hospital and slowly but surely lose weight again until it was expedient for her to be readmitted. Our nerves were constantly jangled and our tempers sorely tested.

How could I possibly think about my own inner struggles when my beloved daughter was swinging between life and death? Of course, her problems must have originated in my actions. I deprived her of her mummy for three-and-a-half years. It was my fault, of that I was certain at first. I did all within my power to assure her of my love and commitment to her. But it made no difference. The illness had moved in and set up house in her body, and no amount of soothing talk, loving attention, apologies, treats or firm boundaries seemed to shift her firmly rooted and totally irrational ideas. My own "stuff" must be put on hold. But that plan didn't work. Pushing pain further away only serves to make it harder to live with. I became increasingly depressed and it became ever harder to cope.

But I knew how to pray a little by now, and also had that deep conviction that everything would be all right. Somehow God would be seen and be real – his light would come dancing and streaming into our lives. I knew it would happen. I would, as always, just have to wait.

We lived on an incredibly tight budget so, in order to earn some much-needed money, I had started my own counselling practice. While we were living in the flat I had taken a couple of counselling courses and now had a Diploma in Counselling and a Certificate in the Psychology of Counselling. With those, the brief training and experience I received in the States, and the many training events I was attending, I felt competent enough to take on private clients. Later I achieved other counselling diplomas. I genuinely loved the work and loved the hurting women (and occasionally men) who came to me with their pain. Their honesty and willingness to change and grow inspired me to press on in pursuit of a lifestyle that included joy and freedom – something that had, as yet, escaped me. I was, however, absolutely sure that it really was possible to live in a state of what Jesus called "abundant" life. I just hadn't found it yet, that's all. "I will, I will," I thought, "I am sure that one day I will."

Among the issues that my clients were facing was that of dissociation. I met with and listened to the stories of many alters; I shared their pain and understood their struggles as far as I could. But I had a secret, of course. I still had a whole family of alters in my head, and from time to time they made themselves known to me in very loud ways. As Amy became more unstable, unpredictable and irrational so the alters became more vocal in my mind. What could I do about it? I was now living forty miles away from Judy and could no longer afford the cost of counselling, never mind the petrol to get there. I would have to cast myself yet again onto God, for I knew no other way of coping with the heavy burden of living. It appeared that I had failed miserably as a wife and mother – hadn't I deserted them in order to seek my own comfort? Hadn't I caused great mental distress in my own daughter resulting in a serious and life-threatening illness? I couldn't even bring in a decent wage as I was not trained in anything other than counselling or Christian work, neither of which paid its way. And anyway, I was too tired and weary to work more than a few hours at a time.

Nevertheless I ploughed on, completely ignoring JuJu or Stormie in their regular tirades in my head, demanding I pay attention to them. I then found work teaching job-seeking skills to the long-term unemployed, then moved on to a residential home for the mentally ill. I was able to cope when I needed to – dissociation served me well. But always I was so, so tired. Not only did I not sleep, but I seemed to live in a constant state of nervous exhaustion, and panic was never very far away. An odour of fear seemed to pervade my life in every nook and cranny. Several times I found myself in the doctor's surgery, not having any memory of getting there, it being the nearest place to safety I could find at the time, and the receptionist would fit me in as soon as there was a space. My GP was kind and gentle even though she clearly didn't understand what was happening to me. I have vague memories of pacing up and down her room in agitation, stuttering my utter confusion and despair – over my daughter's illness, my inability to make it better or to cope with her frightening outbursts; of my sense of devastating loss that I couldn't comprehend, and the shear hopelessness of my life. I felt outside the reach of normal love or good feelings. Just a blob of pain.

She did all she knew to do, and gave me antidepressants and things to help me sleep. When things got really bad I took tranquillizers too. I was referred to a psychiatrist, who told me she could do nothing more to help me other than inpatient care – just a sticking plaster. My heart seemed to throb with grief, for the life I didn't have, for the life I had messed up, for the life I should have had but somehow missed. "What a complete mess you've made, Carolyn. This is not the expected outcome of being a good girl. You've done it wrong. You've just done it wrong."

It dawned on me that I needed to be linked to God through others, as I had been in California. An opportunity followed soon after. I was asked if I would begin a group, in a village fifteen miles away, for people who are suffering from or recovering from a mental illness. Many who come out of hospital feel isolated from mainstream community and family life; they often have few friends and no job or meaningful occupation. I was delighted with the prospect of creating a fun and safe place for these people. They deserve better, I thought, than further trauma caused by loneliness and boredom. What they need is community; a loving, caring, safe group of people among whom they can feel a sense of belonging and with whom they can experiment and expand their developing social skills. Then it dawned on me that I could learn something here about my own healing and journey out of my bleating, baaing, bellyaching place of discontent.

The love and understanding John and I had was good and real but somehow it missed the mark, did not reach the depths of my pain. I longed for connection. To be understood and to understand; to be known and to know. Within the clubs we started, called Friendship Clubs, were many vulnerable souls who no longer (if they ever learnt at all) hid behind the mask of self-sufficiency. They knew they had needs and that they could not make it alone. Of course they couldn't. Nobody can. The motto I repeated to my counselling clients also at that time was: "You alone can do it but you can't do it alone." We have to do what only we can do – make our own decisions etc, but none of us can manage without the support of caring, vital, heart-touching, renewing relationships.

That is what I also needed to hear. I knew I could make it. I knew I could. "Yes, I can, I can!" though at this stage I had no idea how that would happen. I also yearned with every fibre of my being for others to share in the journey. I was lonely. Oh! I was lonely. It had been such a long haul. Would anybody, ever, have any idea what life is like for someone like me?

Chapter
16

Renewal

I still had alters, that's for sure. But I was beginning to realize that they could teach me something about God and the Church. Each alter personality had a common goal and raison d'être, namely my survival. They didn't all realize that though, and so were at odds with each other much of the time. So I continued to be fragmented and divided.

So it is with us all. Lonely. Fighting our battles alone. When Christ comes he opens our eyes to both our uniqueness and our common goal – yes, to glorify him and enjoy him for ever as the Westminster Catechism says, but also I think, to be one, linked together in a harmony that celebrates our separate colours, flavours and traits. Then we are free to be ourselves and so free to merge into one body, yet still retaining and enhancing what each of us are. We are individually the temple of the Holy Spirit. I was one person, many alters; the Church is one body, many parts. Different in function but one in essence.

For some time I had held a vision of us each appreciating fully those who are different from ourselves, particularly those we regard as less fortunate, less educated, less sophisticated, less able. In our "less – more" mentality we are making judgments that are divisive. My vision was for Christian people to see themselves as equally as needy as the bag-lady on the street and as gifted as their favourite hero; to be able to say to the paraplegic "I need you" and to the schizophrenic "teach me". Perhaps that was borne out of my own recognition that every alter, however annoying, dysfunctional or despairing, was completely necessary for both my survival and completion. Was this a picture of the church – of community in completeness? Like a great cosmic jigsaw puzzle each of us fits together in Christ to form the complete and perfect portrait of Jesus. There is a place, a role, a space only I, you, have a right to occupy. For the love God has for me is mine alone, and the same applies to everybody.

Something miraculous and astonishing happened around this time. We were, as always, struggling to make ends meet. While attending a short counselling seminar a fellow student I hardly knew told me she felt it right to give me a cheque, would I mind? I was thrilled, and humbled at her willingness to give to a person she had only just met; she knew very little about me. When the cheque arrived we were blown away – it was made out for ten thousand pounds! Wow! God doesn't do things in halves! We took a much longed-for holiday in Egypt – we still think of it as the best we have ever had – and there was enough to supplement John's income and keep our heads above water while I did unpaid work developing the Friendship Clubs.

Something was going right. Maybe I was, at last, being a good girl.

But not for long. The seeping, creeping depression was moving in slowly but surely like black tar furtively flooding an unsuspecting plain. Each time I looked more of my life was being affected by its grim and sticky pollution. I was sinking in it, and it felt that this time there was nobody there to rescue me. Christopher was a long way away; Judy was not accessible and I felt totally alone with my mysterious mindset offering unlimited opportunities for misunderstanding.

John was always there in the background, occasionally trying to understand what I might be experiencing but mostly simply getting on with his life. He was not the person to sort me out – I needed him to be a husband, not a therapist. He was a great father to my children and a faithful breadwinner. He provided the normality that kept the routine going and my head on the mundane things. He wanted to talk about the children or TV programmes or the weather. He was the healthy reminder that life actually kept moving outside of my muddled head. I did not want him to change his role any more than he did, we were agreed on that one.

Attempting to find anyone who may understand was so risky at this point that I dared not try. I was, once again, the divided self: hopeless and frightened, but also an optimistic leader with vision and plans. My head felt as though it was being broken in two.

In the summer, on the way home from a wash-out holiday in Somerset, John and I had a rather nasty car crash which had totally unnerved me. The car was a write-off, and we were both badly shaken and suffered whiplash and shock. "Something wants me dead, I know it. I should not be alive anyhow, I have been very, very bad. I have told the secret and now I am paying for it" was swirling round in my mind. Meanwhile I had been experiencing more disturbing panic explosions. They would begin with a feeling of agitation and I would have the phrase, "I don't know what to do, I don't know what to do", hurtling round in my head like a frenzied spinning top. I would try unsuccessfully to settle to some meaningful occupation but to no avail. Once again I was visiting the doctor's surgery.

In the autumn John and I had another week away. Amy was at college, even though she was badly underweight, and we had left sixteen-year-old Luke proudly in charge of the house. There were, of course, instructions. Don't walk through the house with muddy shoes (our carpets throughout were pale beige); lock the doors at night; put out the dustbin on bin-day; eat a proper meal at least once a day (the freezer was full); and you can have two friends (only) to sleep over.

We arrived home at midnight from our coach and boat holiday in Germany, tired and glad to be home. As soon as I opened the door I knew something was amiss, there were large muddy footprints on the carpet all the way through the hall and up the stairs. Come to that, there were rather a lot of muddy marks on the paintwork and, yes, the walls too. We found other odd things. Some of my clothes were in John's wardrobe and some of mine in his. Our bedroom window wouldn't close properly; there was a girl's sock under our bed… what on earth had been going on? Luke was in bed, but in our perplexity and desire for answers (things were beginning to look a little dodgy) we went into his room. Unsurprisingly, he wasn't asleep (waiting for the storm?). It turns out that "having a couple of friends over" quickly got out of hand and one thing led to another, with people he never intended to include turning up. It took me a whole week of cleaning, including the hiring of an industrial carpet cleaner, before the house felt acceptable again.

This was the straw that broke the camel's back. "That's it. I can't take any more," I thought. "Everything's going wrong. I can't deal with the alters screaming in my head; with the black depression keeping me awake in spite of tablets; with a sick and irrational daughter, an unhappy husband, a son I can't trust."

Still the wider family didn't trust me. Still I was seen as weird and misunderstood. We were in debt, I was getting more and more tired, more and more depressed, and oblivion appeared rather attractive. Even the challenge of the

Friendship Clubs could not blot out the depression. Down the spiral I plummeted again; somehow I could no longer self-talk myself back into a good place.

One Sunday a pastor came to speak to our church about an organization I had never heard of before, with the name of "Freedom in Christ", first founded in the USA by Neil Anderson. I was not really listening to the talk. When chock-full of blackened weariness it is hard to listen to deep things, you have to just concentrate hard on what is necessary for life, then get on and do it. There is no space for the luxury of pondering; the cut and thrust of living is about all you can handle. But something struck me about this man and the woman who came to give her testimony. They both seemed so happy, in a relaxed, laid-back kind of way. They oozed calm vibes that hit me where I needed to be hit. So I summoned up the strength from somewhere to speak with the lady. She was kind, and – well – hopeful. I did not bargain for her insistence on my talking with the pastor though. I knew he would want me to enrol on his programme or read his book or whatever. I was right. Sort of.

Ian was very gentle. He listened to the woman's interpretation of what I had hinted at – that I was at the end of my rope. Well, she got that bit right. I felt embarrassed. Ian, the pastor, told me that he was a trustee of Freedom in Christ, an organization new to the UK that supports churches in discipling their members. Through this organization his church had been trained in helping Christians connect with who they are in Christ, and lives were consequently being transformed. He and his church could help me, he said. In fact he seemed to suggest that there was a simple way through to complete freedom from all my anxiety. He obviously didn't understand where I was coming from. I tried to explain: "But, you see, I was badly abused as a child."

"Oh, that's no problem, Jesus can deal with that. We will help you."

"No, but it's not as simple as that. You see, it was satanic. Evil. Ritual abuse. That's pretty bad. I've had all kinds of help but things still feel really horrible."

"Oh, that's not hard for God. I've heard of satanic ritual abuse. I'm sure we can help you through that."

"Bless him," I thought, "what a sweetie. But he just hasn't got it at all. I'll try again." Out loud I said, "No, but you see, it was so bad that my mind fragmented. I have…" and I paused to whisper, "Multiple Personality Disorder. That takes years to heal, if ever. I am at my wit's end. I just can't cope with life any more. I am ill, my daughter is ill, we have no money, we've just had a car crash, everything is going wrong. I know we are cursed. I can't carry on like this. Nobody can help me now."

"Oh, I'm sure there isn't anything there that God can't put right. We can help you, I know we can."

"I just can't believe this guy," I thought, "what do I have to say to put him off! He really seems convinced that he and his people can do something for me. I daren't believe him. I daren't. Supposing I'm disappointed? I couldn't handle that."

I politely wrote down the phone number he insisted on giving me, with no intention of ringing it, and went home.

There was no improvement in my circumstances. I was begging God to bring some relief but it seemed as though all fight in me had seriously dwindled, and along with it my hope of life ever becoming more than this slog. Amy was very weak and refusing to eat enough even to maintain basic activity. Her actions and attitudes were still difficult to live with or understand and she would accuse and fight us with such vehemence, such hatred and poison, it seemed as though she had turned into someone else. Where was my darling, sweet-natured, fun-loving little girl? Who had stolen her and replaced her with an angry, bitter, defensive stranger?

John was, as always, the steady presence, troubled and worried but not swinging in the passions of the moment as I was. He carried on his daily routine with little variation and any fears he had he kept well concealed. But I had more than fear to deal with. Sleep took flight even with medication. I was wading through each thick, black day on a tide of sickening exhaustion buoyed up by the mechanical energy of will power and adrenalin. I hated myself. I hated my life. It was only the hope that things will one day get better that kept me going.

But I *knew* deep in my gut there was more to the Christian life than this. I knew that abundant life was my inheritance, not this sham. This is all humbug! No! I will not just lie down and give up. There are people to help. There is beauty to find. There are folk who would like me if only they knew me; if only I knew them I know I could give them something that would enrich their lives. Perhaps there are those who would even understand me. I was sure that one day my heart would sing.

God was at work.

I did, after all, make that phone call to Ian's contact. I was linked up with a couple from Ian's church, Steve and Zoë, who were, as it happened, also pioneering the Freedom in Christ work in Britain. They sounded very confident that my problems could be resolved. In fact I had never before come across such boldness in the face of the intensity of the things I presented. They were positively bursting with excitement about what God could do for me. I was definitely sceptical. Anyway, we set a date to have what they called a "freedom appointment". I had no idea what it was, though I am sure they would have explained it to me. All I heard in my foggy and desperate state of mind was that somewhere out there was some hope that something would change for me. I had all but given up.

The run-up to the freedom appointment, known as the "Seven Steps", was grim. Zoë sounded so kind and positive on the phone, I dare not believe it was genuine. It had been so long since I had held any real hope that things might change. She told me to ring her and Steve every day! "They surely don't mean that," I thought, "they will soon get fed up or overwhelmed with the tangle that is me and then go away." So I didn't ring. But they rang me! What struck me was that they were in no way frightened by what I told them. I had to admit to them that the pages of the Bible were going blank when I tried to read, and the screaming in my head got to fever pitch if I even thought about praying. JuJu was whining all the time; I thought I would go bonkers unless I let her express herself somehow. I was afraid of what they, the alters, might do if I didn't give in to the pressure of their needs, and I was afraid of what they might do if I did. It was catch twenty-two.

The day of the appointment was a very ordinary one. I had slept the night before amazingly well for me – several hours – and felt nervous but not afraid. (Had somebody been praying?) I had no great expectations because I knew that I had tried everything and been disappointed. I was greeted with such joy by Steve and Zoë that I wasn't quite sure what they wanted from me. Even before I got out of the car they were in the church car park smiling their welcome. All a bit fishy. I was introduced to a very gentle lady, also called Carolyn, who was there to pray for the whole proceedings, and sat down with a hot drink. I was handed a book and it was explained that all I had to do was to read the prayers out loud and tick the boxes that applied to me. Easy-peasy.

I couldn't do it.

The first step we did was, it turned out, the last one in the book, and all about my family line; curses and such that I had "inherited". Things were getting stirred up. "I don't like to think about my family. I don't have a family. I don't want to talk about family. Family is not good. Let's do something else. I don't want to do this. No, let's not do this. Please, let's not do this." I was getting stirred up; unpleasant things were happening in me.

Then we tried step one. All about things we have been involved in that were not from God. Like occult stuff, and dark stuff, and things that go bump in the night. That pressed more buttons than I can tell you. I don't actually remember much because I, Carolyn, had gone. When we started to mention things that Satan initiates I was out of there, I wanted to scram, skidaddle, take flight. JuJu came, and others. I don't really understand all that happened that day but I do know that something very, very significant took place. I went home knowing that a turn in the road had been made, I was facing another direction.

I got stronger. Even if the depression did not lift immediately something had been released and I felt freer, bigger, enlarged in my mind.

About this time I had become strong enough to think that perhaps I could, in some way, prevent harm coming to others in the way I had been harmed. I would never, ever want anyone to go through what I had endured and still wrestled with. Supposing the group that hurt me was still in operation. It all happened a long time ago, but people continue to do these things; in fact if anything, there was more scope for abuse with the Internet vastly increasing the ease with which perpetrators can communicate and cover their tracks. So I made the decision to tell my story to the police so that they were aware that in a particular part of the south of England a group had been abusing children in this way. I also felt that it was right to tell them who was involved as far as I could remember. Several close members of my family were clearly implicated, and while I would not choose to cause harm, neither could I live with the possibility that children were still being abused. I needed to be sure that this was not the case.

I was both surprised and gratified when the police took my allegations seriously. CID were called in and treated me with courtesy and consideration; I salute them for their grace and sensitivity. They worked on my case for eighteen months during which time their investigations completely validated my story. Even though nobody was taken to court the one relative still alive was arrested and put on the child abuse register.

I had been advised by doctors to give up my job with the Friendship Clubs and concentrate on finding some emotional stability. I was told not to keep trying to push the boat out, but to look after myself; in other words, to concentrate on being ill. I wrote in my journal:

> I choose to disobey those instructions. I care too much about the members, and others like them, who haven't yet had the chance to be part of a Friendship Club, to give up this work. I care too much about myself to give something up that brings me such enjoyment, fulfilment, challenge and growth.
>
> I believe God can work miracles.

This new hope, this fresh strength was not coming from me but from God in me. The Steps experience had loosened something that had held me for a long, long time. Something was happening. God had heard my cries (he does, you know) for I was once again journaling and the entries were positive:

I must relearn to trust God. There seems to be something of a gentle awakening going on in me toward him and I am so, so pleased. I must listen for him and follow. I must not waver. I must not let the questions hold me back. I must resolve to do what I know must be done – pray, listen, read and obey the word of God, stay close to him and his people. Old stuff but good stuff.

I began to have a series of meetings, every few weeks or so, with Ian, Steve and Zoë. They encouraged me to kick out of my life, out of my thinking, all the lies that up until now I had believed, and hadn't even recognized as lies. They urged me again and again and again to choose to believe the truth about who I really was as a child of God. They taught me that God had already done everything necessary for me to have abundant life. I already had all I could possibly ever need for a fulfilled and joy-filled life. It was mine for the taking. The stumbling block was my ability to receive it, and the real key was to get rid of the sin in my life.

No, there was no sense of judgment or criticism here, just the fact that wrong attitudes and selfish, misguided thinking can prevent us from taking advantage of all that God has given us in Jesus. I readily admitted that I could not believe I was totally accepted by God just the way I was. There must be some catch. Sure, I believed that God loved all people, but somehow an exception would have to be made for me, because of the really bad things I had been involved in. I surely have to be a good girl if I want God to really love me.

Chapter
17

Resistance

My thinking did not change overnight. I worked hard at learning verses that told me how good God is, how much he loved me, and how great is his ability to keep his promises. Renewing my mind in that way was helpful, but only scratched the surface. There were rumblings deep down within my psyche. It was all very well for me to learn verses, but the alters could not be ignored.

Steve, Zoë and Ian, sometimes with Carolyn, Sara (another free and stable member of Ian's incredible little church) or Ian's wife joining them, coped valiantly with my other "parts". Each time we met, which was only every few weeks or so – nothing like the intensity of therapy – we would begin by asking the Lord to show us what he wanted to do that day. He always did! They soon met JuJu, Stormie and Meg (who invariably whipped off her shoes and socks, attempting to make a quick exit). The reappearance of the alters in a public way was both disconcerting and an enormous relief. I had become like a pressure cooker ready to whistle, and it was great to be able to take the lid off and allow them opportunity to express themselves. "I've come. It's just JuJu," JuJu would announce, as if anyone needed that information!

This time, however, it was different. Steve was not asking them to tell their stories. Nor was he wanting anything from them. On the contrary, he and the other members of the team had something to tell us: Jesus has already set us free from the effects of the past, that's what the cross was all about. Each alter could choose to believe that for themselves, and relinquish the burden of carrying around the pain and guilt. Then they would be free from all the bad feelings.

The biggest battle was the realization that the Satanic forces which had driven those people to hurt me in the first place were not going to allow me to heal and grow in Christ without a fight.

I remember little about much of the next few months as the alters were clearly enjoying their relationship with Steve and Ian in particular. Their progress in understanding the way God sees me, and consequently them, was pivotal for my healing. These men very quickly came to understand the dynamics in play in MPD and were able to treat each alter who appeared with respect and dignity. They spoke to the child parts in age-appropriate ways, even allowing them on occasion, to play. But never did I feel that I was bulldozed out of the picture, or that I was just an "interesting case".

It helped, of course, that I was able to explain how it all works and why they needed to be here at all. But I entered into a new place as the focus ceased to be my healing and was fixed firmly on the person of Jesus Christ. He is the only one who can heal, and so I was encouraged, urged, cajoled and pestered at every turn to connect with him and find everything I needed in his presence. It was irritating, frustrating, angry-making and completely liberating. At last I was released from the never-ending search for the right person or the right technique. I was not going to find the right "approach" to me that would bring complete health. I could stop searching and start to gather around me all the benefits I have from being a child of God. It is a bit like the "count your blessings" approach gone mad. It was not a matter of looking at what I have instead of what I haven't; rather, it was looking at what I have and realizing that the "haven't" list doesn't really exist. Having realized what I now have because of what Christ has done for me on the cross, I could scoop them all up, claim them as mine, and enjoy them. The fact is, I always have had all of these things, I just didn't quite believe it, not really, not deep down. I had given mental assent to it, but it had all seemed too good to be true.

However, a new faith was being born in me. I wrote in my journal:

> It is wonderful to begin to feel the stirrings of excitement about the things of God again. It's been such a long, long time. Spiritual issues were so old, so stale, so out of touch with my life. But it feels as if there is still hope for me in terms of having a vibrant, relevant faith that drives and inspires me. At long last I am thirsting for more, and have met a group of people I can relate to at that level. So refreshing. I just want to be with them.

I was encouraged to study the truths of who I am now in Christ. I had to undergo a complete mind-renewal. I had some lies firmly entrenched in my brain – we called them "strongholds". I thought, for a start, that I was not loved, not really. And, of course, I was a bad person. Underneath all the good works was a black soul, and I was busy whitewashing all the time. So the Martha part of me was forever "serving". I dared not allow the Mary part to sit at Jesus' feet and do nothing – that would make me a selfish, lazy person, not a good girl at all. All of my learning and conditioning from a tiny infant onward had led me to believe that in order to be really acceptable I had to "do". I had turned into a human doing and never allowed myself the freedom to be a human being.

Now these guys had come along and told me to stop all of

that. Stop trying. Stop believing those lies. Stop thinking that I am defeated, that the enemy will get me in the end. Stop assuming that at any minute I would do something really wrong and get thrown away like an empty packet. I fully expected Steve and Ian to get fed up with me. I knew I was a drain on anyone's resources once I began to be honest, be myself, that is, reveal all my parts with their fears and neuroses. But they never did get fed up. I have come to recognize that that was because they never assumed that they were the ones who were helping me. They were not the rescuers. It was not they who would bring relief; it was God. And as he had already sorted it all out on the cross, his work was more or less done.

Now it was my turn. I had stuff to do; not my friends, not God, but me. Not to earn my salvation or anything like that, but to release myself from those chains, for much of the bondage was of my own making. I had some important decisions to make. Did I want to be well? Did I want to be free from the demonic oppression that was clearly motivating and directing much of my life? Did I want to integrate the alters, upon whom I rely to save me from facing the pain of the past and from uncomfortable emotions? Did I want to learn what it means to be a responsible, well, whole, no-more-excuses adult? Tough questions but on careful reflection my answer was an unqualified YES!

The process meant that each alter had to make their own decisions, each according to the understanding they were able to reach, of who God is, what he has done for them, and their individual version of repentance and assent. This was not an easy or painless process. There was clearly demonic interference from the start. Steve and Zoë had met with me, and Steve recorded:

We spent most time with Stormie who seems to be a very intelligent twelve-year-old. She wanted to invite Jesus into her heart and we got her to a place where she started to repeat a prayer. However, when she got to a bit about Jesus dying for Stormie, Stormie reacted almost exactly as Carolyn did when we took her through the satanic abuse renunciation: a lot of shouting "no, no, no", talk of blood and some obvious pain. This was to my mind clearly demonic. Anyway, when we got her back, she was able to ask Jesus to come into her heart before passing out.

It felt like a battle from the beginning, and that is, of course, what it was. We are, after all, in the middle of a war. The powers of darkness were clearly not going to give up their domination over my mind without a struggle.

Steve wrote:

I am left with a sense of the enormity of the task. One of the enemy's schemes in both her and us is to try and convince us that it's "just too big" – in a way I take courage from this, sensing that perhaps we are not too far from a breakthrough when the whole of the enemy's works in her will come tumbling down like a pack of cards. God has accomplished so much in her in the last four months and he is not about to stop now.

Trusting these people was a bit risky. Supposing they left me when things became too bizarre for them. After all, they are not getting paid to help me in the same way that Christopher or Judy were. They were free to back off at any time. Having begun to let them into my horror story, could I survive if they were to go? It would mean they would be taking some of it with them, and it is mine. As painful as it is, the memories, the feelings, the alters were all sacred. I felt that if somebody went away having first shared in some of it, it would feel as though a tender section of me was being wrenched from me.

I am so, so glad they didn't go – they stayed. *They stayed!* And I stayed intact.

After Stormie came to the Lord, Meg did, but all was not well. There was definitely something demonic going on. One day we reached the crunch point. It was time I admitted to having secret contact with demons. There were times throughout my life when I felt so close to evil that it became not only quite attractive but positively preferable to turn to Satan than to God. I seldom mentioned it in my journal and never to other people. But my heart was divided. It is easier to connect with whatever feels closest, even if it comes from the pit of hell itself, and I had succumbed many times. So I paid the price – a divided heart and a mind oppressed.

There was a way out, and an opportunity to choose to do that came when we put aside a whole day. We met in Ian's little church – normally a safe and happy place for me. Ian and other kind and trusted friends were present. A confusion of alters came and went, threatening to harm me, and foul-mouthed demons spoke of filth and violence. We had learnt before that the entrance point of a demon had come when I was dedicated to Satan in the blue flame ritual. I had to make a choice. If the demon was to leave permanently I had to choose to renounce the ritual and tell it to leave. Other people could, of course, do that for me; my new friends would have willingly, but the battle was not theirs, it was mine. The struggle was enormous. Everything in me resisted it; it felt that I was saying "no" to part of me, that in renouncing that evil being I was denying myself something I really needed.

My body hurt with the pressure of that moment. My bones cried out to just give in to the evil, that it was easier that way. Forget all about this Christian stuff, the fight was too hard, it was all too hot and too much for me. I felt that if this evil presence went there would be nothing left of me, because it was holding everything together. It felt too powerful and too big for me to even try to resist. The whole of me would crumble if I denied it's place in my life. But I knew in my heart that I could never seriously put demons in the place of Jesus Christ; I just had to accept and endure the struggle.

It was a long and sweaty day, with Ian and the others sticking with me in their love and loyalty, though sometimes unsure of what to do. In desperation, Stormie tried to put her fist through a window and all was in panic and disarray inside my head. It was early evening when Steve turned up and took both my hands, maintaining eye contact. He told me, firmly and without room for argument, to renounce the ritual of the blue flame. After some considerable mental squirming I did as I was told, but it was extremely painful. There came a deep stomach pain, like something being wrenched out of my gut, burning and sickening. I was told to tell the demon to leave, and once again the searing pain in the middle of my body throbbed fiercely. It was real, and at one point I could see something evil filling the church where we were, with its wolf-like image and its matted, filthy fur and enormous fangs. There was a revolting stench and I just knew then that I had to resist this thing. But I also felt terrified of what it might do to me.

I made the choice and spoke aloud the declaration that I choose Christ over Satan. Suddenly all was still. The pain went, the throbbing in my head calmed, there was a sense of peace. I waited for the fiery explosion that didn't come. I was, in a quiet and deeply satisfying way, free. From then on I was able to think about becoming whole once and for all. Janey was the first of this last batch to be integrated. At her joining with me I, at first, felt dirty, naked and exposed but it also signalled the beginning of the end as far as MPD went. Not long after, in the safe company of Steve and Zoë, I was able to ask both of the two alters to join with me, so making two less parts separate from the core me. In April we had another session together and it became clear that one alter named Emily May was, in fact, a demon. By now I knew what to do, Steve and Ian had taught me well, so was able to renounce what Emily May was, and told it to go. After a brief but physically painful internal struggle, which I was prepared for, I felt the release. It had gone.

At the next meeting, about two weeks later, Zoë found Meg in the car park when she arrived. Meg was the next to integrate, which she did with little objection – well if the others were happy to do this it must be OK. Elliot, a fifteen-year-old male alter who was created to protect me from the vulnerability of being a female, was one of three remaining alters. He was quiet and thoughtful and rather wary of Steve and Ian: "What's in all this for you?" But after satisfying himself that I was strong enough to handle anything harmful should it come my way he, too, integrated.

That just left Stormie and JuJu. I just could not imagine life without them. Stormie joined me bravely and calmly though not without some trepidation. But JuJu – How would I cope with fear? I had never had to manage fearful feelings in my life. The few times, recently, when they had leaked through to me I had felt overwhelming panic, and just didn't know what to do. "I don't know what to do, I don't know what to do," thrummed and throbbed in my head. I supposed I would just have to learn to take it to Jesus every single time, no exceptions. There is no other coping mechanism. Steve reassured me this is a good thing – but I was pensive.

I did not want to say "goodbye" to JuJu. She was my best friend, it was hard to contemplate life without her. She was the child I was never able to be. She made sure my needs were met when it did not feel appropriate to ask myself. She felt my pain so that I didn't have to. But the day came, and JuJu arrived at the church, together with Maisie and the other dolls she wanted to show Steve, Zoë and Ian. We sat on the floor in a circle, clasping hands, and I thanked JuJu for being such a brave little person, for taking all the bad stuff so that I didn't have to carry the burden of it. Then I invited her to become a real and lasting part of the core "me". I felt a brief but painful thrill of shock and revulsion run through my body and then the calm. No more cries and whines in my head. No more injections of pain or panic. JuJu is now an irreversible part of who I am.

Minutes after JuJu's integration I had an urgent need to play. There was a cupboard full of toys in the church annexe. How could I resist? The preschool jigsaws were so colourful, with pictures of farmers and tractors and flowers, they were just asking to be put together. I settled myself down on the floor amid the puzzle pieces and toys and felt great content-ment – the warmth and joy of the immediate moment, much as a small child will block out everything but the task in hand.

John did not understand all that was happening, but when I shared things with him he was supportive and loving. I increasingly appreciated the patience with which he stuck with me, waiting for me to emerge into wholeness.

MPD is only an accentuation, a caricature if you like, of how we all are deep down. We hold parts of us that still have child-needs: for affection, attention and reassurance; also a great unrecognized need for pure, uncynical, innocent fun; for play that has no ulterior motive to compete or overpower or mock another. Play for the utter joy of it. Joy for joy's sake. Joy-play is revelling in your own creativity or wonder; in exploring and discovering; in the sheer excitement of curios-ity itself.

JuJu has given me a valuable legacy, not all of which I can

appreciate publicly. I still notice things like a man's Adam's apple bobbing up and down when he speaks, somebody's sticky-out ears or the hairs on a lady's chin. Respectable adults do not see those things. Nor can I stare when someone's cardigan buttons are done up wrong or make castles out of the mashed potato on my plate and I am certainly not allowed to jump in splishy, splashy puddles so that my shoes and socks are covered in the wonderful brown puddley-mud. I am, however, allowed to feel the pleasure of the scratchy bark on a tree, have a finger game with the small child in front of me in the check-out queue, or stare for a long time at the bright colours in a shop window simply for the joy and wonder of the variety or brilliance of the colours, not because of any monetary value. I can chortle and giggle and play (in a totally adult way, you understand) as long as I am in the company of those who know me, who understand that I am really an OK person!

June heralded a milestone to be remembered for ever. Steve, Zoe and Ian came with me as we visited the scenes of much of the abuse. The beautiful, thirteenth-century church with its ancient graveyard was our first destination. The belfry, with its thin ropes hanging through the ceiling, were particularly challenging – I struggled to stay rooted in the reassurance that it all happened a long time ago, that I am now free to see it as a past thing, sorted and over, just a vague bad memory amid so many good ones rapidly being created in my new-found and overflowing life.

We walked out into the sunshine and after a bit of exploring found the flat gravestone by the gnarled old cedar tree under which first Meg hid, then Ashes, before she was put into the newly dug grave. (That was the time of the burnt sacrifice of what I believed to be my friend.) The scene was horribly familiar, as even the proximity of the old wooden door into the west side of the church was there. I could see it all. But that, too, was only a past recollection. Nothing to get hot under the collar about. I can decide to see it for what it is now – a lovely old churchyard set in the heart of a picturesque and leafy village in rural southern England. The sun was warm on our backs, the birds were singing in the green canopy above, the weathered grey stone of the church looked settled and content in the mid-morning quiet. Around me were people I loved and trusted. The bad stuff seemed a long, long way away.

I sat on the once-hated flat, stone grave. That's all it was, a slab of stone. I perched on the edge to chat to my friends. It felt cool and rough, pot-marked with age and patched orange with lichen. I then climbed right up on it, and sat cross-legged on the top like a little elf. "I am not afraid of a bit of stone; I am not afraid of what once was and is no more; I am not afraid of the past. Jesus has rescued me from all of that. Because of him, all because of him, I am loved and wanted today; I am secure and significant today. I am free!" Steve recorded: "An enduring memory for me will be seeing her sitting there very much at peace with a big smile on her face. When I think about all that the Lord has done in such a short space of time it's absolutely amazing. Thank you, Lord!"

It certainly felt that a great deal had taken place in the eight short months since I first met these people and had a "freedom appointment" – the seven steps to freedom that Neil Anderson outlined. I was learning that all I needed in order to be totally free was already mine. That's the whole point of the death and resurrection of Jesus: to win my freedom; to make it possible for sinners like me to connect, totally, with the living God and receive his life. Abundant life is real – and I was beginning to taste it. I felt like Dr Who's Tardis: bigger on the inside than on the outside! In fact I could barely contain the huge expansion of love and joy inside. I am not talking about feelings so much as facts. Those good things, and more, were actually dwelling and growing in my life.

I no longer have to live in a state of constant apology for who I am and what I am doing wrong. I am, present tense, a forgiven and redeemed child of God! That has to be good news in anybody's book. Therefore I can, I *really* can, live in the light of that good news. I, Carolyn, have been set free from the bondage of past terrors.

There are, of course, consequences to what has happened to me. I still have some physical problems, particularly ongoing fatigue that may have been caused from living on high doses of adrenalin when I was very young. I am also very small in stature due, I am told, to the early trauma. I failed to thrive as a toddler because when I should have been experiencing a happy growth spurt I had to be on high alert, anxious at a very deep part of me. I am still tiny – I can buy clothes to fit an eleven-year-old. But I feel no bitterness, just gratitude that I am alive in God, though I do feel occasional frustration that I cannot talk to people without getting neck ache!

I have forgiven my abusers and feel no need for revenge or aggression. That is freedom! The walk into forgiveness was not as onerous or difficult as I expected it to be, and has brought a relief and joy that only the absence of guilt can. Though all my abusers that I am aware of are now dead, I can look at their photographs and feel no hatred or anger whatsoever.

I no longer have to find my identity in what other people did or did not do; in what happened and how I reacted to it; in how good or not I was. I can now find my identity in what God has done for me, and therefore who he has made me to be.

The Bible came alive in a way it never had before. I had always found it riveting, powerful, sometimes attractive, sometimes repellent because of the conflict between God and the demonic in my life. Now that the conflict, though still echoing in my head on occasions, has been largely dealt with due to my better choices, I can boldly immerse myself in his word knowing that it is the truth with a capital "T". It is the truth that applies to me, today. It is the truth that will, and has, set me free.

I later went through the Steps a second time, this time being in full control the whole time without the alters coming and going. I was, for the first time in over forty years, able to make choices that were totally mine. There was no demonic interference, and no conflict of interest between me and my other parts with a different agenda. Not that it was easier the second time round. I had to make hard choices.

I was coming to realize that much of the quality of my life depends mostly on the decisions I make today, and cannot be blamed on what happened to me yesterday. I can choose to believe God or not. I can choose to accept his forgiveness and be glad in it, or not. I can choose to forgive others and so be released from the bitterness and burden of holding grudges, or I can spend a lot of energy maintaining the hate and resentment. I can even decide to love, to be humble, to repent, to live in freedom or bondage. It all comes down to what I choose.

Philip Yancey writes: "A believer prays, and heaven responds; a sinner repents, and the angels rejoice; a mission succeeds, and Satan falls like lightning; a believer rebels, and the Holy Spirit is grieved. What we humans do here decisively affects the cosmos." I am *not* insignificant. I am a child of the most high God, and my choices matter.

A big issue for me was whether to continue to believe that I would die soon, at any time, because I had done the unthinkable and told my story. I had let the big secret out, I had snitched, grassed, informed. Now, my gut told me, I was in for it. It was payback time. Somebody, something, somewhere, will make sure I suffer.

But those were all lies. They had been in my head for a long time, so of course they were pretty much part of the fabric of my being and thinking. But I was wrong. Those thoughts did not come from God, they were not true; they were old ways of thinking that had been drummed into me when I was very young. Because I now belonged to God the evil one could no longer touch me. I was now safe. Time to ditch those ideas, time to kick them into touch, stamp on them, say "boo" to them and replace them with reality: I am totally safe. I am not going to pay the price of death for sin, neither mine nor anyone else's. God has already done that; there is only room for one on the cross, and Jesus was that one. There is no need to pay what has already been paid. So it is now safe for me to believe that I don't have to be a "good girl". What a relief!

I had spent so much time and energy trying to be good. I had lost so much sleep, used so much stamina, wasted so many years doing all I could to be a very, very good girl. But I was never good enough. I thought, therefore, that I deserved to die, and so, ultimately, now that I had done the very worst thing, and told the story of what really happened to me, I would surely die. But, guess what, Jesus came into my life in a new way and reminded me that that is what his sacrifice was all about. I don't have to sweat and strive any more. I don't need to ever be JuJu again, and worry constantly that at any moment I will be punished by rejection and death for not being good enough. What a wonderful, wonderful thing it is to be free from that! Glory! Glory to God! He has done it! He has been the "good girl" for me!

Chapter
18

Rejoicing

I was forty-six-years-old and starting all over again. I had to learn a completely new way of coping with my emotions, many of which were totally new to me. I had never really learnt how to deal with fear, or anger, or frustration. Usually I could unobtrusively click into another personality and didn't have to grapple with anything like self-control or submission to the Lord. I had to become like a child again, learning how to integrate those daily emotions that wanted so badly to take over my being. The only way I knew – dissociation – was now no longer an option. I did, however, know that I had choices. I could think what I wanted to think.

It was easy, however, for me to hand over my thoughts. A kind of reflex swung into action when things got difficult, and often I found myself in the grip of a spiritual conflict. Demonic forces were eager, I suspect, to reclaim my mind and took advantage of every opportunity. But there was comfort: "I have told you these things," said Jesus, "so that in me you may have peace. In this world you will have trouble. But take heart! I have overcome the world" (John 16:33).

I had begun to tell parts of my story at the Freedom in Christ conferences around the south of England. Steve and Zoë were so very supportive, and so were the rest of the core team at the time: Mike, Clare and Sara. Without their encouragement and infinite patience I would have crumbled in doubt and confusion and old ways of thinking. But they poured out the consistent and strong message that I was doing OK, that God would use me, that I was accepted for who I am, not for what had happened to me.

Giving my testimony was a mixed blessing. Being able to stand boldly in front of a church full of strangers and proclaim that Jesus has set me free from the bondage of terror and lies was exhilarating. On the other hand, as soon as I stepped down from the platform something changed. My head became full of old voices, telling me that I am really, really bad; that I should never have done that; that I am a liar and deserve to die. The torment, in the early days, would drive me to think about cutting myself in order to effect my deserved punishment. I don't think I ever acted on that, but the impulse was extremely strong. My mind had been so programmed to think in those ways that it would take some firm and persistent "renewing" before my thinking came into line with the truth. Of course I hadn't done anything wrong – I was proclaiming the truth about the deliverance that any child of God can expect (though it takes a different form for each of us). Of course it is OK to tell of God's wonders. Of course, of course... but my mind was still running along the old grooves.

There was a conference held in St Andrew's Church, Chorleywood, not far from London, and the atmosphere was one of faith and strength. About 150 people were there, eager to learn and ready to soak up what we offered them. The atmosphere was one of joy and excitement. When it was my turn to speak I, a little nervously, walked up onto the stage and, after sharing about counselling and how the Freedom in Christ approach fitted in to that arena, told my story. As soon as I had finished, even though I could hear the applause, see the smiling faces beaming their encouragement, the torment began. Nothing could drown out the deluge of condemnation flooding my mind. The clanging, jarring abusive thoughts were loud and real; the scene of happy, responsive people in front of me darkened and receded into the distance. I felt as though I was being attacked by a swarm of angry bees and they were all I could hear and feel. Somehow I got back to my seat and Mike was there ready with a supportive hug. "I have to go, I have to get out of here, I have done something very, very wrong. I don't know what to do, I don't know what to do."

As the session had ended for a tea break I was immediately surrounded with people. Would I please talk to someone in distress and urgently in need of counsel and reassurance? "Right, I must put my own stuff on hold now. It's time to focus on someone else. This is the time for dwelling in the shadow of the Almighty, not for dwelling *on* self-pity." Pushing the angry bees into a corner of my mind and throwing myself onto God and into the task of comforting another, I was able to get things into perspective. I spent time with the hurting person and after they had heard the truth and was able to connect with it a little I could look at my own battles. Mike and a few others were there for me, surrounded me and prayed.

I had learnt something valuable. I can manipulate these bees. I have power over them. They are just thoughts, that's all, they are just old ways of thinking, old lies. They are just a scheme of the evil one to discredit what God has actually done for me. I can pay attention to them and be dominated by them or I can ignore them and banish them. The choice is mine. Wow! That makes me quite powerful. What once had the power to bring me down to the dust, to shrivel my faith and shrink my confidence, no longer has that effect. As long as I am part of the vine I have his authority and can command all that is evil to go. It works; the power invested in us in the name and authority of Jesus really works! Raymond Brown writes that "Empowered by God, the smallest of grasshoppers can give giants a rough time" (*The Message of Numbers*, BST Series, IVP). *This* grasshopper was turning up the pressure!

As time went on I was to learn that lesson many times. Often I would feel the familiar condemnation, and many times I would ring Steve and whine about the bad feelings. But gradually, gradually it dawned on me that I didn't need to run to someone else when things got hot. I could go to Jesus, look first at him, and then make my choices. I could choose to believe the truth and banish wrong thoughts from my mind. If I suspected there was something evil or demonic behind it I could command it to go. And lo and behold, it would! Sometimes I needed the affirmation of someone safe, and went to Steve or one of the team, but little by little I grew up.

I am still growing. Still working out who I am. The person who was born seemed to have disappeared a long time ago. I don't even have her name any longer – I wasn't "Carolyn" until fairly recently. I was known by another name, the one I was Christened with.

Life is now very, very different. Everything has improved. I appreciate and love my husband more than ever, love my children in a way that is free and without pain or guilt. I so enjoy my family and many friends. I now also revel in the ministry the Lord has so graciously and generously given me to share.

When I first spoke of my experiences at conferences I would have a long string of people wanting to share with me their own story, or the struggles of someone they love. We became aware of a very real need for guidance and support for churches that are trying to help someone who is deeply wounded. Often these hurting people have done the rounds of church ministry teams, counsellors, clinics and hospitals. They had all been looking for that special approach, that new technique, that anointed person who would pray or counsel and say exactly the right thing, and all would be better. Rather like a lottery – would the right word come out of the barrel this time that hits the spot, that lessens the pain? For most that never happened.

We decided to devote a portion of the Freedom in Christ ministry to helping churches and Christian leaders understand the dynamics both of the deeply wounded individual and of their path to freedom. The gospel is big enough to embrace even the most "damaged goods". Jesus is strong enough and powerful enough to breathe healing into the most hurting of souls; and because it is him and not any person, the search for the "right "place, person or approach can be replaced with a healthy realization that each hurting individual has his/her own responsibilities in the healing journey. Instead of looking to others, they need to look to their own life; to examine their own beliefs and mind-sets and see if they really are in line with what God has taught, commanded and instructed. If you think wrong thoughts – believe lies – then you will have negative emotions that reflect those thoughts. Those strong and uncomfortable emotions will dictate your actions and your actions will in turn lead to a dysfunctional – and unhappy – lifestyle.

I began to write down some of the principles that had helped me in my release and growth in faith. When Christian leaders contacted the office they were put in touch with me and I would speak to them about finding some structure for their own "deeply wounded person". I spoke of taking them through the Steps and then bringing together a whole team of helping, loving people (who are themselves working on their own freedom and maturity) around that person. It is in community that I think God brings the most lasting healing. Then comes the long-term but fruitful walk as together they all discover the truths that will unlock the doors and windows in our minds and allow the bad stuff to be thrown out, and the good stuff to take root in the rich and nourishing soil of godly faith and security.

FIC decided to take me on as a staff member so that I could devote a portion of my time to this promising work. I felt so privileged, if not a little daunted. After all, I was still working on my own "strongholds", which reminded me constantly that I am still a "work in progress". But my life was becoming newer and fresher and more Technicolor by the day! It was still springtime for me, and I was free for the first time to step out boldly into the unknown knowing that it was safe and I was safe. Perhaps God really has given me something I could offer to others. Wow! If he can do that for someone like me, he can do that for anyone!

At times a church group would come to visit me, or I would go to see them. We would talk about the issues that their particular individual struggles with, and the best way that their team could support them in replacing the lies they had believed with the truth. Sometimes it was necessary for me to speak about ritual abuse and perhaps even explain the dynamics of MPD. At other times the problem would be an eating disorder, depression or addiction. Sometimes the hurting person just couldn't cope with the demands of life. Either way the approach and the answer was still the same. The symptoms vary widely, but it is not the symptoms that we are treating. The disease is basically the same and so is the treatment, with appropriate adjustments made to suit each individual situation.

Most of the work is done through email and phone conversations, when the response to a difficult situation can be rapid and relevant. There have been results. Good ones! People are appreciative: "What you said was a real help (as usual). Thank you for being there in the way that you are. It's just wonderful and so much appreciated by us all."

"You showed me that there is always hope for hurting people."

"Your thoughts were very helpful and encouraging. Thank you for being so available to chat and, beyond that, even making yourself available now. We really appreciate that."

"Thanks again for all your encouragement."

One church leader's wife I was helping had been supporting a lady struggling with alcohol abuse and self-harm, and who had a history of horrific ritual abuse and was DID (Dissociative Identity Disorder – the current, more accurate name for Multiple Personality Disorder). One day she wrote to tell us that her abuse survivor had integrated all her alters, had reunited with her husband and was now a happy and thriving wife and mother, free of the pain that had dogged her for years. There had been no "therapy" or expensive counselling, just obedient, patient and faithful Christian people around her who were prepared to believe that God could be the whole and lasting solution to her seemingly insurmountable problems. Change did not happen overnight, nor without a struggle, but come it did.

Within two years three DID ladies whom churches were supporting with this approach were completely integrated. Two of them are now actively involved in the support of other SRA/DID victims. One anorexic young woman, after many hopeless years in the mental health system, was able to leave hospital and thrive in the embrace of a church support team, using the FIC principles. She was well enough within a few months to get a job and become a fully involved member of her church and community.

Another lady who had suffered childhood abuse and never really trusted the members of her caring church found a sense of safety and trust as a structure of support was put in place for her. They used the steps to help her understand the reason life was so difficult for her. Great strides were made in her maturity, healing and quality of life. One woman, who was still carrying around with her an abusive and unhappy past, gradually realized she is pure and special for the first time in her life, could let go of the past, and felt like celebrating. She had a caring group of people around her to join in her rejoicing.

There are lots of lots of these struggling folk. Many of them have done the rounds of counsellors and conferences. They have thrown themselves at those they perceive could help them, often being met with suspicion or even rejection because of their lack of social skills or the persistence with which they pursue their goals.

These accomplishments seldom happen quickly, or without struggle and crises. My job in Freedom in Christ is to be on the end of the phone and email to encourage, teach and support these churches as they support and encourage their wounded person. They will take the person through the Steps to Freedom and help them in every way to walk in that freedom. As I write material to assist these churches, I am reminded again and again of how the Lord has used caring, patient people who dare to believe that God is big enough to meet every kind of need, even when they could not understand them and could see no obvious way out.

What a privilege and pleasure it is to be able to reassure these leaders and supportive Christians that there is a way through for the deeply wounded. It involves boundaries and a firm structure; it involves identifying the lies and dealing with them; it involves actively growing in the knowledge of the truth as they undergo the process of "renewing their mind"; and it involves the body of Christ consistently reminding them in every possible way and in every possible circumstance that they are loved and forgiven by an infinitely patient and powerful God. Our lives involve him at every point, in every detail.

I now head up a whole team of people who are trained in supporting churches. Two members of that team were part of my own support network when I was still grappling with alters and demons and the strongholds of lies in my own life. Sara and Carolyn have stuck around and now can speak with confidence of what God can do in someone's life, for they have seen him do it for me (and in their own lives). We are now looking to run workshops where we can teach these principles to church groups, and spend quality time helping each group apply these truths to their unique situation.

There have been those in my own life who have reassured me, stuck with me and, yes, really loved me in the name of Christ. But most of all there were those who, like Steve and the FIC team, have been prepared to tell me over and over and over again that now I had to make the decisions. They taught me that it was not they who could heal me, it was not technique or right combination of prayers and counselling that would set me free from the shackles of the past. But it was God's actions in Jesus, and a decision, a whole trail of decisions, that I had to make to believe the truth of what he had done and give up the dependence on old ways of thinking, lies, that were clearly wrong according to God's way of looking at things. That meant the onus was on me. That meant they had to have the courage to leave me in my pain sometimes, until I made the right choices, until I connected with God myself rather than rely on someone else's prayers.

Ultimately we cannot believe or repent or forgive for somebody else. We have to do those things for ourselves. No matter how painful it is to watch, we have to keep our hands off if we want to see the captive set free, and we must allow them the dignity and privilege of experiencing the power of God themselves, just them and Jesus. We must point the way, love them, support them, love them, encourage them, love them, affirm them, love them, teach them, love them. But when all is said and done, Jesus longs to form a deep and real relationship of freedom and joy with them, and we do well to allow that to happen without our interference.

There are many facets and levels of living. Abundant life is one in which the sky is not the limit, God is, and he, of course, has no end. We need to keep our ears cocked and ready, alert to the prompting of the Spirit, to the direction of the call of God. He will surely beckon us, like Aslan did, to go further in and higher up. We will hear, if we are still enough for long enough, we will catch the faint call, which becomes louder and more sure as we turn our face towards him. Just as the "piper at the gates of dawn" beckoned Ratty and Mole, so we find ourselves invited, drawn, welcomed to a place of unimaginable joy and abundance.

> "It's gone!" sighed the Rat, sinking back in his seat again. "So beautiful and strange and new! Since it was to end so soon, I almost wish I had never heard it. For it has roused a longing in me that is pain, and nothing seems worthwhile but just to hear that sound once more and go on listening to it for ever. No! There it is again!" he cried, alert once more. Entranced, he was silent for a long space, spell-bound.
>
> "Now it passes on and I begin to lose it," he said presently. "O, Mole! The beauty of it! The merry bubble and joy, the thin, clear, happy call of the distant piping! Such music I never dreamed of, and the call in it is stronger even than the music is sweet! Row on, Mole, row! For the music and the call must be for us!"
>
> (Kenneth Grahame, *The Wind in the Willows*)

"The music and the call must be for us." Yes, it is, it really is. But hearing it depends on whether or not you are tuned in, linked up, connected. I had, for years and years, adjusted my emotional and spiritual antennae to that which was negative. I was waiting at every turn for condemnation and judgment, and when it didn't come became suspicious. "No condemnation" is surely too good to be true. It is all my alters knew – the expectation of punishment and dire consequences.

But then I was taught that there was another frequency, that of acceptance and significance and security. It belonged to the God of the Bible who says that I am for ever loved and now cleansed through the sacrifice of Christ. I can readjust my spiritual tuning mechanism and listen for the distant piping of joy, of the clear call responded to by the angels who constantly worship at the throne of the Lamb and by those of us who love to hear the name of Jesus. God's big word is not "No" but "Yes". Now I can. Now I am. No longer trapped and in a dark, tight place, but as I dwell in him who is my "strong tower" I can survey the land before me and realize I am in a broad, expansive place; a place of springs and flourishing growth. How blessed I am! How blessed are all those who choose to believe the truth!

I love my husband and children deeply, and in turn I know that they love me. Amy and Luke have both flown the nest and are making a life for themselves – Luke in ministry in the North, and studying to be a youth worker, Amy, now on the right side of health, working with children in the South, and studying for a qualification in children's ministry. Both are still coming to terms in their different ways with the years apart from mum, but are growing and learning. I am so proud of them. John continues to be the patient, steady, down-to-earth, non-judgmental rock that he has always been. I am deeply grateful to him for sticking by me even when he did not understand or fathom what was going on in his wife. His love has been tried and tested and found to be real and solid, founded in him who is love. I also appreciate my sister and her family who have been only a distant part of my story but who I have grown to love in a new way. I have such a wonderful family.

God has done more for me than I can ever thank him adequately for. We value our times together as a family and I am grateful too for the wider family, in spite of the pain some have caused. Most have been hard-working, loyal citizens who, without fanfare or praise, have lived out their quiet lives kindly and thoughtfully. Some have even made a wider mark on the world. My only regret is that more of them haven't responded to the love of the Saviour who forgives and releases. I am also eternally grateful for the many who, in the name of Jesus, offered a cup of water, a bucket, a whole deluge to a wounded and hurting victim. She has been and is being made whole. I am glad to be who I am, and glad to be able to share with you the story of how I was bound and fragmented and full of fear, but now I am free!

> My chains fell off!
> My heart was free!
> I rose, went forth
> And followed Thee.
> (Charles Wesley)

Proclamation

It is possible to live. Really live.
It isn't just an illusion –
    that smile of Goodness,
    that balm that soothes wounds of grief
    etched deeply onto a tattered life
    of tired hopes and frayed dreams.
It wasn't just imagination's futile groping after purpose,
With that longing to be known.

No, it is real. Real!
A fleeting glimpse of purity rises from my ashes of despair.
Flying free on wings of mercy,
Carrying a shout of joy through a thousand corridors of
    sadness –
Echoing into infinity the bold proclamation
"El Shaddai reigns.
Almighty God reigns forever!"
Overwhelming Love washes light into dark, cold memories
    of shame.
Cleansing secret feelings,
Mending tender, broken heart-strings.
Creating a new song:
A song of adoration.
A song of triumph.

The music of eternal beauty
Mingles with the sweetness of Passion's fragrance,
In the majestic dance of worship.

It is real. Real!
No longer do I dare to whisper words of praise,
But proclaim, in a voice sure and steady
Ringing down through the ages,
Heard above the myriad angels' song –
"El Shaddai reigns!
El Shaddai – *my Father* – reigns forever!
Alleluia! and Alleluia!"

Afterword
Steve Goss
Freedom in Christ, UK

I was privileged to be part of that small church team, led by Pastor Ian, who helped Carolyn as she went through the final stages of her long healing process. I had no idea what I was letting myself in for! However, I wouldn't have missed it for the world. Apart from getting to know a very courageous lady, we all learned an enormous amount.

I hope I can encourage you by sharing briefly some of what we learned together with a few of the questions the experience raised for me and the conclusions I have drawn.

Is DID real?

It was Ian who originally made contact with Carolyn and then asked Zoë (my wife) and me to take her through the "Steps to Freedom in Christ", a tool we had recently found highly beneficial in our own walk with the Lord and in our church. We had never used it with someone who had deeper issues.

At the time we were also setting up an office for Freedom In Christ Ministries in the UK. God had given us a clear call but it felt a strange thing for us to be doing. Before coming into contact with Freedom In Christ's teaching, I had never counselled anyone in my life, and I would run a mile from anything remotely connected with spiritual warfare. It was just not my cup of tea at all. I felt I just wouldn't know what to do or say.

Although a "freedom appointment" is usually run by people of the same gender as the person going through it, Carolyn had expressed a preference for a male presence as her American therapist had been such a help to her. A married couple seemed like a good way forward and we also had with us a prayer partner (curiously also called Carolyn!). Carolyn had informed us that she had suffered "satanic ritual abuse" which had led to "Dissociative Identity Disorder" (DID). I had no real idea what these things were and contacted the American office of Freedom In Christ for some advice. We received some helpful explanations (which didn't exactly lessen our feelings of trepidation!) but, in retrospect, the best advice we received was from Hal Parks, "Don't worry – Jesus always turns up!" It was on that basis that we found ourselves waiting to meet Carolyn at the time scheduled for her appointment.

She was a little late arriving but when she did, I was immediately relieved. I don't know what I was expecting but what we got was a smiley, chatty lady who seemed entirely normal. I asked her to explain a little about DID, which she helpfully did, and then asked her what we should do if one of her other personalities appeared. "Don't worry," she said, "I'm sure that won't happen."

The appointment started completely normally with Carolyn saying some prayers. However, it didn't take long for her to find that she simply couldn't say the words. She was clearly in some kind of pain caused by emotional or spiritual issues. We persevered, praying hard. She battled on slowly (very slowly) and painfully.

Then it happened. At one particularly difficult moment, it was as if someone had changed the software or flicked a switch. There was a momentary closing of the eyes and when they opened she appeared to be someone else. She looked different – wide-eyed and shy. She spoke in a very different voice – a child-like voice. Her mannerisms became those of a small child: lolling on a chair, swinging backwards and forwards, standing on one leg. She had a coy smile. She introduced herself timidly as "JuJu".

What do you do when a forty-something lady you hardly know starts behaving like a five-year-old before your eyes? Well, I may not have known much about counselling or spiritual warfare, but I did have young children and knew a thing or two about speaking to them. I took a mental leap and spoke to her, rather tentatively at first, as if she were a young girl. It seemed to work. We forged a relationship. She eventually told us what was bothering Carolyn and Carolyn then "came back" and was able to deal with the issue.

That set the pattern for future sessions with Carolyn. When memories got too much for her, she would "go away" and someone else would "come". We lost track of how many personalities we met but each of them was a distinct personality with a distinct accent and distinct mannerisms. Each of them seemed to have a special task, a set of specific memories that were being safeguarded because they were "too painful for Carolyn". Some of them were so young that they could not speak or had to ask for explanations when we used long words; others were older; most were female but one was male; some were very disturbed; a few seemed to be very rounded personalities.

It felt completely bizarre. Part of me was wondering whether this was an elaborate hoax, whether we were simply being taken for a ride. I decided early on that, even if this were the case, this lady clearly needed to find her freedom in Christ so it was worth continuing! Yet as we met with Carolyn over a longer period, it became quite obvious to me that there was no way she could be "putting it on". If it were an act, it was so good she deserved several Oscars.

We grew to realize that the "alters", once they got to know and trust us, were helping the process along. One of them, in particular, took to calling us at home. You could practically guarantee that during the course of the conversation she would tell us what the particular issue that Carolyn needed to deal with next was. So, after that initial session, we found ourselves meeting with Carolyn every few weeks or so (not something we had anticipated) and sitting down with her as she brought some very difficult issues to Jesus and dealt with them.

I came to understand that DID is a God-given defence mechanism, a way of protecting her from the horrific abuse she had suffered (and, let me assure you, she has kindly spared you most of the nastier details of the abuse).

The team felt led to work with each alter and lead them individually to the Lord and then celebrate Communion with them. Of course, Carolyn was already a Christian so there was no actual act of salvation going on here. I think in a way it is similar to when any of us get to a new point of commitment and yield another part of our life to the Lord.

As the alters "integrated", it became clearer than ever that they were all just part of one personality that had fragmented for self-protection. Whenever an integration happened, we could clearly see the mannerisms of the integrated alter in Carolyn. She was literally becoming a "whole" person before our eyes. In no sense did the alters disappear – they simply became part of the whole person.

I have no doubt whatsoever that Carolyn's DID was a genuine condition. How loving of God to equip us with an extreme defence capability so that we can survive even the most horrific abuse.

Was this simply a mental issue?

If we had treated this simply as an issue to do with Carolyn's mind, we would not have made much progress. We'd have gone round and round in circles. Why? Because we were also dealing with the demonic. When you are solemnly dedicated to Satan as a child and forced to take part in all sorts of nasty rituals, it sets up some points of influence for the enemy in your life!

It became apparent early on that the alters we met were being controlled in some way. They would say that they were "not allowed" to do things like pray or read the Bible but would not tell us who was laying down the law. Sometimes taking Communion or other spiritual things caused a very violent response quite out of keeping with the gentle lady we had come to know. One evening I took a phone call from someone I didn't recognize who said, "Leave her alone. Or I'll burn that ****ing church of yours to the ground." The number the call came from was Carolyn's. We also received a letter through the mail from an alter we'd been told about, but never met. Her name was Emily May and she was apparently an older lady. It was written in an elderly lady's handwriting style and commended us for trying our best but assured us it would never come to anything and that Carolyn would never get better. It ended rather chillingly, "Leave her alone!"

We began to wonder whether Emily May really was an alter or whether there was something else going on. We got our answer one evening. Carolyn rang in a distressed state and told us she had tried to integrate Emily May and all hell had broken loose.

"Emily May" was a demon who had gained entrance to Carolyn's life during the satanic rituals. It was exercising quite a lot of control over the way Carolyn and her alters were thinking and, consequently, over Carolyn's behaviour. I don't believe for a minute that Carolyn was "possessed" – she was a Christian and belonged to Jesus. Satan could never have her back. However, all of us can leave "doors" open in our lives to the enemy's influence (see Ephesians 4:24–26). Carolyn had more doors open than most and consequently more scope for the enemy to influence her. She was also used to handing over "the levers of her mind" to another part of herself or sometimes, as it turned out, to a demon.

In retrospect, progress was quite slow up to the point that Carolyn learned to deal with the demonic. The turning point came at a session with the team at which I was not present. Carolyn had become violent and abusive. The only way to restore order was to get one of the alters to "come out" and so she had been, in effect, a pleasant teenage girl most of the day. Every time Carolyn herself "came back", however, she was sullen, abusive and violent. As a last resort, the team tried addressing the demon directly and commanding it to leave in the name of Jesus, but it simply spoke back to them through Carolyn saying that it wasn't leaving because "Carolyn loves me".

It was 7 p.m. by the time I got there and, as I was leading a teaching session an hour later on the other side of town, could only stay for twenty minutes. Carolyn was abusive and disconnected. The teenage alter, as usual, had given us the information we needed – Carolyn needed to renounce a particular ritual during which she had been dedicated to Satan. One thing I had learned through Neil Anderson's teaching is that there is no need to get into a "power encounter" with the enemy where the demon and I battle it out leaving the poor affected person like a pawn in our game. I love Neil's illustration of this – if you have a problem with flies in your kitchen, you could study them carefully, work out where they were coming from and pick them off one by one. What would happen? More would come! Why? Because there's a big, rotten, stinking pile of rubbish attracting them. So what's the best way to sort out the problem – get rid of the rubbish!

In biblical terms, what is needed is simply repentance: "Submit yourselves… to God. Resist the devil, and he will flee from you" (James 4:7). There is never any need to address the demon directly and certainly no reason to get into dialogue with it – after all, what would be the point of trying to get reliable information from someone whom the Bible tells us is a liar?

I knew, therefore, that there was no way I could do this for her. She had to get rid of the grounds the demon had for influencing her. I, therefore, asked Carolyn to renounce the ritual she had been made to participate in. I got a mouthful of abuse in return as she unthinkingly regurgitated the thoughts that the demon put into her mind. I remember saying to her, "Look Carolyn, I've got another ten minutes maximum. It's entirely up to you. Do you want to get rid of this thing or not?" At that point, she confessed that she was scared because she had been led to believe that, without this particular demon, she would die. We were able to show her from God's word that that was not the case. She then did a very brave thing. She renounced the ritual and told the demon to go. She was suffering intense pain as she did so and a look of terror came over her face as the demon appeared to her as a huge wolf-like figure. But she did it!

The main point is that *she* did it. Not me. Not the rest of the team. She had everything she needed in Christ (2 Peter 1:3; Ephesians 1:3). Because she submitted to God and then resisted the devil, he really had no choice but to flee. The only power encounter that needed to happen for Carolyn to be free happened 2,000 years ago at Calvary. No demon is too big to stand against that.

For too long the Church has either ignored the demonic and treated issues as if they were simply to do with the mind, or it's tended to ignore the mind and see everything in terms of spiritual warfare. The Bible is clear that we are whole people – body, mind and spirit – and we need a whole answer. We need to steer a middle path and recognize the reality of mental illness as well as the reality of the spiritual world.

From that point on, Carolyn's healing accelerated significantly. There was still the odd unguarded moment where she handed her mind over to a demon but she quickly recovered and has learned now to take "every thought captive".

What were the keys to Carolyn's recovery?

1. Knowing who she is now

The whole point of DID is to shield the sufferer from events that are too traumatic for them to handle. They see them as having happened to someone else. As Carolyn's alters integrated, the dividing walls in her mind came down and she was able to see memories that were previously hidden. The passage of time had in no way caused those memories to fade. They were strong and real and appalling. Many a time I recall seeing her come to terms with the awful fact that, "That was *me*. They did that to *me*!"

Those kinds of experiences cause you to believe some things about yourself: "I'm dirty. I'm guilty. I'm abandoned." Some of those things were never true – she never was guilty for being abused. Others were true – she really was abandoned.

The trouble is that they become ingrained in our thought patterns and it becomes difficult to think in any other way.

Carolyn would feel dirty or evil. She would feel that she could never escape or that she would certainly die for going against Satan's will for her. Once the spiritual conflicts have been resolved, the hurting person has to do a lot of work on these thought patterns or "strongholds" that feel true but are not.

A key thing we came to understand is that it is not so much the traumatic event itself that causes us ongoing pain, but the lies we came to believe as a result of it. Healing comes not so much by dealing with memories or trying to understand the past but by getting the hurting person to believe the truth about who they are *now*.

So we spent quite some time concentrating not so much on what happened back then but on who Carolyn is *now*: a child of God, holy, pure, loved, definitely not abandoned but someone who can never be separated from the love of God.

Sometimes when she was overwhelmed by traumatic memories of what had been done to her, I would say simply, "So what?" That may sound hard but it seemed to help. It's not that what was done didn't matter – of course it did – but it no longer had any hold on her as long as she didn't fall for the lies it predisposed her to believe.

Underlying the whole process was a foundation that got stronger and stronger in Carolyn's mind that she is now a child of God who can become everything that God is calling her to be.

2. Resolving personal and spiritual conflicts

I don't believe anyone can walk in the freedom that Christ came to bring unless they resolve the personal and spiritual conflicts that allow the enemy to influence us and hold us back.

For most Christians, forgiveness is the major issue. This was true for Carolyn too. We watched as she slowly and painfully forgave those who should have protected her but did not. It wasn't easy. It would have been so much easier to have held onto the hate. But once Carolyn understood that the reason Jesus commands us to forgive is for our sakes and is primarily an issue between us and God rather than between us and the person who hurt us, she was able to make a decision to forgive and forgive from the heart.

The "Steps to Freedom in Christ" is an excellent tool to help people resolve their personal and spiritual conflicts. Once Carolyn had gone all the way through it the first time we met, we continued to use it in one way or another at every session. We always used the opening prayers to start a session and then Carolyn would ask the Holy Spirit to lead her. As he did so, she would use prayers from one or more of the Steps. Having the Steps gave us a very helpful structure to work within.

However, it was, of course, not the Steps that set Carolyn free. It was Jesus.

3. Taking every thought captive and standing firm

Carolyn needed to be determined. She needed to be in the race for the long term. When we first met her, I'm not at all sure she had any real expectation of lasting freedom, but as she concentrated on truth she began to have real hope.

Because of the DID and the demonic issues, she had never really been in control of her own mind. Because she had been a victim and learned at an early age that it was useless to struggle, she could tend just to give in and agree with the enemy when he came knocking with his accusations and lies. However, she really worked at renewing her mind, which meant committing herself with grim determination to believe what God's word says even when it didn't feel true. She learned to realize that not every thought in her mind was necessarily her own and that the question to ask was not so much where it came from but whether it was true. She learned to hold her thoughts up to the truth in God's word and throw out those that did not agree with it.

This is something that she – and for that matter I – need to do all the time. As she has become aware of her particular vulnerabilities, she has developed "stronghold-busters" (simply lists of Bible verses and a prayer based on them) and committed herself every day to believe what the Bible says rather than what her past experiences predispose her to believe.

She has come a very long way.

4. A team of people around her

I hope you've noticed that the person who did all the real work was Carolyn. In a real sense that's how it has to be. No one else can repent for her, believe for her or forgive for her. She simply took hold of the freedom that Christ had won for her. However, her pain was so huge that I suspect she simply could not have done this alone. She needed the encouragement, support and straight talking of the team – and it was important for our sakes that there was a team of people so that individuals did not get burned out during the process.

Isn't helping hurting people just for experts?

None of the people on the team were in any sense experts. None of us had experienced anything like this before.

It would have been very daunting indeed if we had believed that it was in any sense our responsibility to "fix" her. All we were doing was encouraging Carolyn as she made some hard choices.

Please do not think I am saying we don't need those who are specially trained in medical or psychological issues. Of course we do. You have seen how many compassionate, professional people have helped Carolyn along the way and I would never go against, or advise a hurting person to go against, expert advice.

However, let's recognize that if she had not resolved her personal and spiritual conflicts in Christ and known the truth, then the best anyone could do for her would be to help her cope with her issues. The fantastic news is that, in Christ, even the most deeply hurt individual can expect to *resolve* their issues completely and go on to become a fruitful disciple.

It's Jesus who is the Wonderful Counsellor – as we help people bring their issues to him, they receive much more than if they simply came to us. It's so important that the Church recovers this "theology of resolution" or, as I like to put it, a belief that the gospel really works.

Could it happen in my church?

The danger of putting this story in a book is that the people involved suddenly take on some kind of mystical quality. Let me assure you that everyone involved in the team was very ordinary indeed. We all still have our struggles. As we have seen, the real work was done not by the team but by Jesus and by Carolyn.

How lovely it was that Ian, a pastor from a church that was not her own, was prepared to lead a team to help Carolyn. How much better it would be, however, if hurting people were able to find help in their own church. We have come to realize that there is absolutely no reason why that should not happen. In case you think the church involved in this story was a large, well-resourced church, in fact it had less than forty members.

There's one additional reason why this could happen in

your church with another hurting person – and that's Carolyn herself. Her role in Freedom In Christ Ministries is to equip churches to help those who are deeply wounded. She heads up a team who come alongside church leaders and offer advice and guidance as they bring hurting people to Jesus. We've seen many hurting people find their freedom and many church leaders with a new-found belief in the fact that "the gospel really works". It's a delight to see Carolyn operating in a very fruitful and valuable ministry. She never thought it could happen.

One of the core values of Freedom In Christ Ministries in the UK is that the work of setting captives free and ministering to the hurting is the work of the local church. We do not, therefore, offer help directly to individuals who are hurting but work by equipping churches to help them. When I was part of the team, it was as an ordinary member of that church rather than part of Freedom In Christ Ministries. It's a delight to see many hurting people finding their freedom in churches who had previously thought that the issues were "too big" for them and to see the delight of ordinary Christians as they see that "Jesus turns up".

This is the anointing that the Lord shares with us in every local church:

> The Spirit of the Sovereign LORD is on me,
> because the LORD has anointed me
> to preach good news to the poor.
> He has sent me to bind up the broken-hearted,
> to proclaim freedom for the captives
> and release from darkness for the prisoners,
> to proclaim the year of the LORD'S favour
> and the day of vengeance of our God,
> to comfort all who mourn,

and provide for those who grieve in Zion –
to bestow on them a crown of beauty
instead of ashes,
the oil of gladness
instead of mourning,
and a garment of praise
instead of a spirit of despair.
They will be called oaks of righteousness,
a planting of the LORD
for the display of his splendour.

Isaiah 61:1–4

How wonderful that we can expect to see, through our churches, the poor, the brokenhearted and the captives becoming "oaks of righteousness" for the display of God's splendour! It has been a huge privilege to watch as Jesus and Carolyn have gone through that process together.

Appendix A
Christopher H Rosik, PhD

Carolyn Bramhall has written a most compelling account of her incredible life journey. I consider myself quite privileged to have been alongside of her for a small but important portion of her story. Honest psychologists will acknowledge, as I readily do in Carolyn's case, that we often receive as much if not more from our patients than we give back to them. She was one of my first cases of Dissociative Identity Disorder (DID – formerly known as Multiple Personality Disorder). I was a few years out of graduate school at the time she showed up at the Link Care Counseling Center seeking help. I had not even heard of the dissociative disorders in my training. Yet what confronted me was a young English woman reporting a number of bizarre-sounding symptoms and regularly losing consciousness in the waiting room. Carolyn's situation, along with a couple of other severely distressed patients I was seeing, forced me to a make a decision. I would either stay in the emotionally comfortable confines of my training or educate myself in the controversial area of dissociation, which seemed, from what little I knew, to make sense out of Carolyn's symptoms. I will never regret my decision to step, no, really leap, out of the box and into the indomitable depths of Carolyn's mind and spirit.

If in reading Carolyn's story you sense that there were many twists and turns, you would be absolutely correct. I have often compared the work of treating DID to running a marathon. Perseverance is a key ingredient. There were many opportunities for Carolyn to despair of ever healing. The frequent sudden losses of residence, the ongoing financial uncertainties, and the agonizing departure of her family for England were just some of the many adversities she faced in being a stranger in a strange land. But just as often there were many small and some rather large indicators of God's gracious care for her. An anonymous gift of money or food, an encouraging word from a Christian friend and the gentle but noticeable movement of God's Spirit in her life often seemed to have a timing that was surely from above. I give Carolyn great credit for never forgetting to look for these signs. They kept us going even when we could barely see a step ahead.

Carolyn's journey is so rich with lessons for survivors of childhood trauma that it is hard to know which ones to highlight here. Nevertheless, there are a few points I believe stand out. The first has to do with the validity of the diagnosis of DID. When I first began to consider Carolyn's symptoms as aspects of a dissociative disorder, I had the good fortune of being relatively unaware of the controversial nature of this diagnosis. I did not approach her care with any more or less caution (read skepticism) than I did with any other psychological condition, and therefore perhaps was more able to accept her experience on its own terms. Exposure to DID has a unique ability to threaten our pre-existing views of human consciousness as a unitary entity, and hence it can create very emotional reactions in both the church and psychiatric communities (Rosik, 2000).

However, in the past fifteen years dissociation has gained wider acceptance among professionals who work with trauma, where it is understood to be an extreme form of post-traumatic stress reaction often associated with disorganized parent-child attachment patterns. Studies that have attempted to validate DID patient accounts of childhood abuse have found high rates of confirmation for "ordinary" traumas and lower rates of verification for ritual abuse accounts. Thus, in my estimation, there is little convincing evidence that DID sufferers are merely suggestible people who are making up false memories for attention. Most report they have been aware of at least some traumatic recollections since childhood, although it should be acknowledged that even these memories are encoded in a manner consistent with childhood cognitive development and as such can represent the trauma with a mixture of historical, symbolic and fantasy material. It is therefore very important that the matter of how to understand traumatic memories be left to the patient and not usurped by counsellors, pastors or friends.

Perhaps the most troublesome and potentially harmful issue concerning the spiritual care of DID patients is that of exorcism or deliverance prayer. The crux of the problem is the significant overlap among the symptoms Christians consider to be related to demonization and the indicators of DID.[1] This has resulted in many persons with DID experiencing harmful expulsion rituals as well-meaning but uninformed ministers attempt to expel a part of the individual's mind. My experience with patients has convinced me that great care must be taken in assessing and comprehending potential dissociative psychological dynamics in any one who is being considered for exorcism or deliverance. As Christians we are commanded to "test the spirits" (1 John 4:1), and it surely plays into the enemy's hands when an alter personality is misinterpreted as a demon.

That said, I would also be hesitant to uniformly rule out a potential role for exorcism-oriented rituals in the healing process of DID. Certainly Carolyn's experiences as well as those of a few other patients I have seen suggest that prayers for deliverance or expulsion are not inherently harmful when conducted in a sensitive and informed manner.[2] Our experiences also indicate that Dr Neil Anderson's "Steps to Freedom in Christ" is one approach that can be adapted to the work of treating DID and reduce the incidence of spiritually abusive prayer when patients present with concerns regarding demonization. I suspect the polarization that exists over this topic is fuelled by the lack of a shared experience base between the two sides. Specifically, just as therapists (especially secular ones) rarely if ever encounter people who report being helped by expulsion-oriented prayers, so too Christian leaders are just as unlikely to hear back from those who experience their exorcisms or deliverance prayers as damaging.

Another critical lesson that should be learned from Carolyn's story is the necessity of both psychological and spiritual care in the treatment of trauma-related disorders in general and DID in particular. I sincerely doubt whether Carolyn's spiritual needs would have responded so well to the "steps to freedom" ministry without the foundation of emotional healing and stability that had been facilitated by her earlier psychological counselling. By the same token, I also suspect there would be no duration of psychotherapy sufficient enough to bring wholeness to her mind without the assistance of pastoral care that made possible deep freedom in the spiritual realm.

The glue that holds all of the psychological and spiritual interventions together for healing is the DID patient's sense of acceptance by and belonging to a larger community.[3] Patients connected to a supportive social network tend to make progress in their healing more readily than those who are isolated from others. This is why the Church has such a crucial role in the lives of Christian DID sufferers and other trauma victims. It can either be an agent of tremendous healing through God's grace and comfort or it can be a source of great hurt and despair when the patient is misunderstood or condemned. Carolyn's life has poignantly demonstrated the truth of this statement. Pray that God would grant his shepherds the wisdom to do better in their care for these most wounded of Jesus' flock.

Finally, I think it's worth addressing a question that I often hear from my patients and one which I am sure you may well have thought while reading Carolyn's story. The question usually is stated something like, "If God is so powerful, why doesn't he just make my mind whole immediately? Why must healing take so long?" While I would never pretend to know the mind of God, my experience with DID and other childhood trauma patients suggests that the answer may have something to do with the premium God places on truth. If we are his disciples, Jesus says, "Then you will know the truth, and the truth will set you free" (John 8:32). Jesus, of course, is the personification of this truth (John 14:6). Yet might it also be possible that each of us are, through this truth, called to become increasingly aware of our own personal truth, including the aspects of our childhoods that may have been too painful to acknowledge or remember at the time? If genuine healing only occurs in the light of a conscious awareness of truth, then it seems possible to understand the prolonged healing process as an expression of God's gracious care. Severe childhood trauma survivors would be overwhelmed and retraumatized were God to suddenly release into their awareness all the truth of their heretofore hidden spiritual, emotional and physical pain. This would not lead to wholeness but to further psychological fragmentation. God would risk becoming another abuser were he to grant such a patient's prayer for immediate healing.

Yet God is in the business of healing, and works to bring this about for his children according to his perfect timing. Carolyn's life makes this abundantly clear. I trust that in sharing her story, Carolyn has brought encouragement and hope to you as well, whether you are a survivor or a survivor's spouse, friend or minister. Whatever your current circumstances, never forget that your life journey is also of vital importance to God, who wants to guide you even now. "For I know the plans I have for you," declares the Lord, "plans to prosper you and not to harm you, plans to give you a hope and a future" (Jeremiah 29:11).

Notes

1. Rosik, CH, "When discernment fails: The case for outcome studies on exorcism", *Journal of Theology and Psychology, 24*, 1997, 354–363.
   Rosik, CH, "Some effect of world view on the theory and treatment of Dissociative Identity Disorder", *Journal of Psychology and Christianity, 19(2)*, 2000, 166–180.
2. Rosik, CH, "Possession phenomena in North America: A case study with ethnographic, psychodynamic, religious and clinical implications", *Journal of Trauma and Dissociation, 5(1)*, 2004, 49–76.
3. Friesen, JG, Wilder, EJ, Bierling, A, Koepcke, R, & Poole, M, *The Life Model: Living from the heart Jesus gave you*, Can Nuys, CA: Shepherd's House, Inc., 1999.

Appendix B
Carolyn's selected alters
(Based on notes made in 1992)

The capable adults

JULIE   Age 35
Created age 2. Host personality. Front of normalcy. Mostly denied abuse. Had overall control most of the time. Equilibrium increasingly broke down as alters revealed themselves. Biggest struggle was accepting diagnosis and the existence of the alters. Relied heavily on Carolyn and J.C.; often doubted she was a person at all. Function: to maintain cohesion.

CAROLYN   Age 36
Shoulder length wavy hair. Wore soft colours, usually a primrose-yellow flowing dress. Gentle. Smelt nice. Laughed a lot. Loved children. Creative with play and crafts. Sensitive, kind, thoughtful. Knew most of what went on internally. **Function:** to comfort, console, care for all on the inside and especially the "children". Also able to cope on the outside when calm and normalcy was required.

NB All the alters, plus Julie, ultimately integrated into Carolyn, the strongest alter, so becoming who I am today. I refer to myself through-out the book as Carolyn, although most people knew me as Julie until 1992.

CHARLOTTE   Age 29
Wore long, dangly ear-rings, bright coloured clothes. Flamboyant. Sophisticated. Confident, intelligent, impatient, opinionated. Enjoyed reading philosophy, psychology, theology. Highly cognitive. Took charge internally in emergencies. Spoke often to frightened or unreasonable alters, with some success. Was adept at writing and could type well. **Function:** to rationalise and explain events.

The children

JUJU   Age 5
Short, dark hair. Clothing usually slightly askew. Often wore red dungarees. Liked drawing and eating Smarties (M&Ms). Loved bright colours, especially red. Open, verbal, expressive but stammered when anxious. Affectionate with people she trusted. Loved to talk to those she felt safe with and would look for ways of prolonging her time with them. However, was highly strung, nervous, fearful in the face of trigger situations. **Function:** to carry extreme fear.

(JuJu was spiritually perceptive and took an active part in prayer sessions. As time went on she grew increasingly calm and trusting and could stay "out" for comparatively long periods of time without panic or overwhelming fear).

BETH   Age 6
Blonde shoulder length hair worn in ringlets and curls. Liked to wear dresses and pretty things, frills and bows. Shy, easily upset, timid. Round, pleasant face, rosy cheeks, slightly plump. Longed to feel good inside. Was confused and found it hard to trust. Suspicious of male authority figures. Was suspicious when promises were made to her as she expected them to be broken. Was left-handed and could write simple sentences in a wobbly hand. Function: to carry anguish, torment, confusion.

ANNIE   Age 8
Was created when I was 5. Thick brown hair, straight, slightly longer than shoulder length. Untidy appearance, mainly because of lethargy due to frequent pain. Little energy. Slept a lot. Largely unaware of outside events. Intelligent and thoughtful. At first was unable to sit up for very long when she came out, but rapidly gained strength after working with Christopher. **Function:** carry memories of physical pain, and sometimes the present pain too. (Bore most of the pain at the births of Amy and Luke so I didn't have to).

(Converted 28.11.90)

ASHES   Age 12
Thin, shoulder length brown hair, rather straggly. Slim, about 5 feet tall. Rather sullen character, in her own private world, felt more at home in woods and among wildlife. Animals responded to her.

Often so distressed she screamed and wailed. **Functions:** to take the pain of a particular memory; identified as a human sacrifice victim; to hold memories of confinement e.g. in church cellar, a coffin, a grave.

LITTLE JOEY Age 2
Wore dungarees too big for him. Large round, blue eyes. Thin, pale, lethargic. Looks slightly uncared for. Sucked thumb, expected ill-treatment. Hid in corners. Liked fishes. Said little. **Function:** to carry sense of victimisation.

MEG Age 4
Short, fair hair. Wide eyed expression. Liked to wear only loose clothing, hated cumbersome things like coats sweaters, shoes and socks, and took them off when she could, in preparation to run. Slim, small and nimble. Short attention span. Uneasy and suspicious. Deep, underlying need for touch and affection. Obsessed with getting away, usually by running. **Function:** to escape from perceived entrapment or danger.

(Meg found it hard to break free from automatic response to run in any difficult situation even when she understood that such action was unnecessary and futile. She grew in her trust, especially of Christopher. Often could sense unease or fear inside yet usually unable to explain it.)

PEGGY Age 4 (Meg's twin sister)
Tall for her age. Usually wore pink. Straight fair hair, longer than Meg, worn loose, with coloured slides to keep it off her face. Bright, alert, talkative, confident. Liked to show off her achievements. Loved to play. Had a fear of monsters, mouths and teeth. **Function:** to play when I was unable to behave like a normal child.

PIECES Age unknown – child.
Extremely frightened and nervous, unable to trust, confused about surroundings, forgot easily. Disoriented, poor vision. Completely broken in spirit. **Function:** to carry memories and sensations of being bound and blind-fold, usually swung in a closed sack prior to abuse, causing severe confusion and disorientation.

(Integrated with Julie at baptism.)

JANEY   Age 7
Very thick, short hair, almost ginger; never tidy; didn't care about appearance. Straight, upright. Curious, liked to touch things, find out how they worked, eager to learn. Hated cold feet and "noises" in her head. Disliked being touched. Liked to play alone with dolls. **Functions:** to carry memories of sexual abuse; to escape through play.

(Janey's abreactive times were vivid and often nauseous to me. They involved acting out the event using dolls, and then lying on the floor and feeling the feelings. This latter part sometimes involved groaning and rolling. It appeared to bring a measure of relief, however. Some therapy times including Janey are recorded on video-tape.)

DIBBY   Age 8
Sturdy frame, strong limbs. A determined little character, with a mindset to battle through all difficulties. Strongly motivated to be well and feel good, clean. Patient. Had endurance. **Function:** to cope with bestiality, sexual and physical acts with animals, sometimes being photographed.

PIPPA   Age 4?
Stubborn child. Repeatedly said "go away", "I don't want to ". Courageous with adults. **Function:** to exert her will against that of the abusers; to object; communicate our will.

CAROL   Age 3 or 4
Very small. Happily and quickly removed clothes. Thought she was pleasing others by doing so. Came out in situations where the perceived need is to please others or when memory work has triggered that response. **Function:** to remove clothing when I was unable to respond to that demand.

VERA   Age 4
Ginger hair. Disturbed child obsessed with sexual acts. Thought that the way to find affection from adults was to make herself available for abuse. **Function:** to obey abusers' instructions.

TIC TAC   Age 4
Obsessed with eating and being eaten. Sometimes known as "Crumpet". **Function:** to hold the fear of being eaten.

"The middle" (surrounded by the "Blue Flame".)

ERICA   Age 30
Named from the heather of the moor that she took us to in order to avoid possibility of detection and rejection. Was uneasy at our being so openly known as MPD. Was spokeswoman for all in the "Middle". Became a Christian in Pete's office. Watched outside events closely and with great interest. Was cautious and took an intellectual approach to therapy. **Function:** to protect from rejection by avoidance.

(Integrated 8.1.92)

MILLIE   Age 23
Continual cry: "Will somebody help me? Will somebody help me?" Was unable to maintain being "out" for any length of time. Fearful and suspicious. Appeared to have been left alone in a field. Was very afraid of and aware of demonic activity. Was a pawn in the hands of the "Middle". Often seemed to be quite psychotic. **Function:** to take and feel weakness when I had to maintain appearance of strength.

SECRET   Adult, female, always same age as Julie.
Would say nothing to reveal truth about the abuse. Struggled with spiritual realities. **Function:** to protect the lie, to maintain my unbelief about MPD and the reality of the abuse. Strongly argued that nothing happened and we had not been abused.

(Was delivered and converted 12.12.91.)

STEPHANIE   Adult, female.
Identified with the object of evil worship. Was told she had special powers and was promised control and special significance, but was tricked. Therefore angry towards Satanists, and everyone else. **Function:** to be trained up to high level in Satanism.

(Changed her name from "Satan" to Stephanie after conversion 18.9.91 in Pete's office. Baptised and became level one alter on 22.9.91 at J.C.'s integration.)

The Invisible Ones
(focused on getting it right and being invisible)

CARRIE Age 17
Tall, thin, fragile. Immaculately dressed in pretty clothes, pastel shades, lace trims, round collars. Clean, well-scrubbed appearance. Quiet, apologetic, fearful, hesitant, timid. Continually assumed she was a nuisance, unclean, dirty. Good at drawing, though denied it. Had big problems with eating, and was generally anorexic due to early incidents of consumption of flesh and blood in ritualistic settings, and of Emily May's domineering attitudes over her causing repression of shame feelings. **Functions:** to carry shame and memories of certain rituals; protection of Little Joey.

WHISPER Age 13
Heavy set with dark complexion, quiet, afraid of being seen. Spoke in whispers. Became a Christian during an evangelism training session. **Functions:** to carry memories of a particular event of sacrifice; to keep us quiet and unnoticed.

The angry ones

J.C. Age 14
Short, brown, wavy hair. Stocky. Smiled only for the people she liked. Disliked too much femininity. Wore T shirts and jeans. Had trouble with spotty complexion. Strong-willed, decisive, compassionate. Cared deeply about justice issues. Hot-tempered, could flair up suddenly. Impulsive. Liked to joke; quick witted. Later matured beyond her 14 years, became less volatile and more dependable. Actively participated in deliverance sessions, grew spiritually and generally stayed close to me most of the time, speaking for Julie when assertiveness was called for. **Function:** to carry anger over the injustice of abuse.

(Integrated with Julie at baptism 6.10.91.)

THE JUDGE Adult male.
Thought initially to be a demon and "expelled" during a deliverance session involving Becky and Michelle, but still existed in less malevolent form. Made judgements on how safe people and situations were for us. Still desired revenge through murder. **Function:** a protector.

MICHELLE   Approx 13
Formerly "Terror". Appearance unknown. Frantically afraid, though not hostile. Hyper-vigilant, especially at night, for fear of demons. Remembered the supernatural aspects of rituals. Until deliverance and conversion almost incoherent in her terror of being overcome by the demonic which she vividly saw. Became more calm and was found to be highly intelligent, precise, with good command of English. A pleasant girl, who liked reading. **Function:** to carry memories of the supernatural, especially at night.

HONESTY   Age 12
Little known about appearance. Open, friendly disposition, eager to please, sensible and level-headed. Trustworthy. Easily upset by my stubbornness to accept truth of the abuse. **Functions:** to deny reality of abuse; carry memories of specific event i.e. marriage ceremony to Satan.

(Delivered and converted 16.9.91)

STORMIE   Age 12
Around 5ft 3in. pretty face when she smiled (which was seldom). Thick brown hair, loose, just below the shoulders. Small features, wore jeans. Angry, impulsive, easily upset. Extremely fearful of going to England. Liked candy, soda, fast foods. **Function:** to initially get me out of England; later to be used by the enemy to bring disruption.

(Stormie grew more relaxed and trusting daily, though appeared to regress in age, and behaved more like a 12 year old girl than her former suspicious adult-like stance. Deliverance and conversion recorded on video tape.)

JUDE   Age 9
Short, unkempt, slightly ginger hair. Hands and knees not too clean. Always had full pockets. Pleasant face. Quiet, defensive, thoughtful. Liked football, stamp collecting, making models. Hated anything connected with women. **Function:** to carry hatred and aggression especially towards women.

PANDA   Age 30
Male. Wore black trousers, white T shirt, black leather jacket. Tall, heavy set, receding hairline. Usually gentle but aggressive and violent when roused. Acted as a "bouncer" on the inside as well as on the outside. Fiercely protective of the alters. **Function:** protector.

Further Help

In the UK

If you are an individual looking for help, in the first instance please talk to your church leader and advise them of the support that Freedom In Christ can give them as they support and encourage you.

Church leaders – take a look at www.ficm.org.uk and, if you feel we can encourage or equip you, please get in touch with us at:

Freedom In Christ Ministries
PO Box 2842
Reading RG2 9RT
UK
E-mail: info@ficm.org.uk

In the USA

Contact:
Freedom In Christ Ministries
9051 Executive Park Drive
Suite 503
Knoxville, TN 37923
USA

Phone: 865-342-4000
Fax: 865-342-4001
www.ficm.org

Other Countries

Details of other Freedom In Christ Ministries international offices are available at www.ficm.org

Freedom In Christ In The UK

Church Leaders - can we help you?

Thousands of churches around the world use Neil Anderson's material to help Christians find their freedom in Christ – often with results that amaze them. If you would like to explore the possibility of establishing a "freedom ministry" in your church, Freedom In Christ Ministries is here to help. We run a programme of conferences and training, we can provide opportunities for church leaders to sit in on freedom appointments to see how it works, and we are always more than happy to offer advice.

Send for our Resource Catalogue

Send for our full colour catalogue of Neil Anderson books, videos and audiocassettes. It includes resources for individuals, for churches, and for local freedom ministries as well as for specialist freedom areas such as fear, depression and addiction. It's also crammed with hints and tips.

Join the UK Freedom Fellowship

If you are using Freedom In Christ materials to help others, join our network of like-minded Christians and receive regular news, encouragement and affirmation. Open to anyone involved in helping others take hold of their freedom.

For details of any of the above write to us at:

Freedom In Christ Ministries (UK), PO Box 2842, READING RG2 9RT

Or e-mail us: ukoffice@ficm.org

"It is for FREEDOM that Christ has set us FREE"
Galatians 5:1

Freedom in Christ is an international, interdenominational ministry whose objective is "to free Christ's body in order to advance His kingdom".

Please note that Freedom In Christ can not generally arrange personal freedom appointments or offer personal advice but works by equipping local churches. We may, however, be able to put you in touch with a local freedom ministry.